VIETNAMESE

COOKING

VIETNAMESE

COOKING

EXOTIC DELIGHTS

FROM INDO-CHINA

PAULETTE DO VAN

Quantum Books

A QUANTUM BOOK

Published by
Quantum Publishing Ltd.
6 Blundell Street
London N7 9BH

This edition printed 2003

ISBN 1-86160-618-4

QUMVET

Printed in Singapore by
Star Standard Industries (Pte) Ltd

Contents

★ Introduction 6

★ Glossary 18

★ Back to Basics 22

★ Soups and Starters 24

★ Fish Dishes 46

★ Chicken, Duck, Frog and Quail Dishes 56

★ Pork Dishes 76

★ Beef Dishes 86

★ Lamb Dishes 94

★ Rice Dishes 100

★ Vegetable Dishes 106

★ Noodles 112

★ Desserts 118

★ Index 126

INTRODUCTION

Vietnam is a beautiful country about 1650km/1025 miles long and, at its narrowest point, about 45km/30 miles wide. It is bounded to the north by China, to the west by Laos and Cambodia, and to the south and east by the Gulf of Thailand and the South China Sea. It has been ruled variously by the Chinese and French and has traded with the Portuguese and Indians; all four cultures have left their marks on its cuisine – a unique cuisine which has also been influenced by the miles of coastline and the many rivers that traverse the country.

Vietnam can be divided into three regions. In the north, where Hanoi is the capital, the food is less sophisticated than in the middle region, which boasts the ancient capital city of Hue. The food of south Vietnam is more refined still, particularly so in the now renamed Ho Chi Minh City, the former Saigon, which was sometimes known as "the Paris of the East"

From China the Vietnamese adopted their love of noodles, the way of cooking, the very healthy stir-fry methods. They discarded soya sauce and invented their own substitute, the ubiquitous *Nuoc Mam* sauce, which has been described by great cooks and poets as "edible perfume". Nuoc Mam is made from fermented fish and smells as you would expect fermented fish to smell. Depending on how far north you go, the smell gets more and more pungent but, when added to food, it does indeed become edible perfume.

BELOW

Tourism is opening up in Vietnam, and the beautiful coastal villages are amongst the many attractions.

ABOVE
The Forbidden City, within the citadel of Hue. Hue is the ancient capital of Vietnam, in the centre of the country.

BELOW
A hangover from the colonial days of the French, French bread is common and is used to mop up sauces and gravy with meals.

ABOVE
A cao dai temple. The eye is the emblem of this sect.

Laos, Cambodia and Thailand have influenced the Vietnamese in their use of herbs. No Vietnamese meal is complete without there being at least two or three fresh herbs present, either as a garnish or in their own right as part of the meal. The Vietnamese love to wrap up their food in fresh lettuce leaves and to include one or two herbs in the parcels; the favourites are coriander, mint, basil, dill and fennel. The Indians and Portuguese brought spices and developed the combinations that came to be known in the West as curries. The French, who colonized Vietnam, forced the Vietnamese to be inventive – under the regime the peasants had to create wonderful dishes from the leftover pieces of animals that were not commandeered by their European masters. It is ironic that in France today, some of these dishes – such as steamed or stewed chicken's feet – now command high prices. The Vietnamese used caramel and glaze to create original tastes and to preserve, but they discovered coffee from the French, together with French bread. At home we would always mop up the juices with hunks of the latter, torn off and passed around. This still holds true today in Vietnam.

Note Several recipes in this book that are specified as "Vegetarian" use Nuoc Mam sauce.

Utensils

In the cooking of Vietnamese food, there are a few kitchen utensils that you are certain to find useful. They are not absolutely essential – Vietnamese food can be cooked using perfectly ordinary western utensils – but they do make life easier.

Wok The first thing you are going to need is a wok. This is a thin, curved pan traditionally used in the East, particularly by the Chinese. It is now coming into its own in quite a few very well-known restaurants in Britain.

The first woks were beaten out of tempered steel to make use of heat efficiently and quickly – they originated in China, where wood and fuel are at a premium. To make them even more efficient, they were curved to fit snugly over the flames of the Chinese brazier. To the Chinese and other people living in the East, including Vietnam, the wok is the complete cooking utensil, used for frying, stir-frying, deep-frying, boiling, braising and steaming.

Woks come in different sizes and are made with different materials. For the average western home, the ideal size is the 35cm/14in wok. It is available in carbon, tempered or stainless steel, and with a non-stick coating. The really hi-tech cook may even have a plug-in electrical wok made of carbon steel, possibly with non-stick coating.

Woks are generally available in the larger supermarkets in kit form, which includes a stand, lid, steaming rack and a multitude of small accessories. You should be careful to get a good, well-fitting lid, preferably not made of carbon or tempered steel as these are heavy and suffer from rust – much better is the cheaper aluminium lid, or a stainless steel one if you prefer.

Some woks have a pair of handles, normally of the same material as the wok; others have just the one wooden handle. If you have a strong wrist the single-handled wok is probably better, but if you are the least bit apprehensive about lifting and tossing around a heavy frying pan, you might be better off with the double-handled wok.

Carbon or tempered steel woks are traditional. Although they are made of thin metal they are quite heavy, and, without care, rust very easily. To prevent this you need to rub them lightly with some oiled kitchen paper and keep them in a dry place. They come with a wax coating which is easily removed by a brisk rub in hot soapy water. The wok

RIGHT

Left: double wooden-handled wok with wok brush; right: single-handled wok on wok stand with long-handled metal sieve and smaller perforated ladle; below: long wooden chopsticks for cooking on chopstick stand and soft brush for cleaning woks.

should be rinsed and dried, then put on a very high flame and allowed to smoke. Pour in a little oil and rub it around the pan, making sure you include the rim as well. Do this a couple of times and then wipe the outside with oiled absorbent kitchen paper and leave to cool. Your wok is now "seasoned".

The Vietnamese rarely wash their woks, so simply wipe yours with absorbent kitchen paper. If you feel the need for scouring, then do it with some salt. When you are satisfied that the surface is acceptably clean, wipe with oiled absorbent kitchen paper. I can remember my father shouting and brandishing his cleaver whenever we dared to put his woks into water without his say-so.

If you wash your wok with soap, you should re-season it as above. It goes without saying that the best way to keep your wok in good condition is to imitate the Vietnamese, who simply hang it in a dry, well-ventilated place.

The stainless steel wok does not have a rust problem and is easier to clean, but it does have a couple of disadvantages: it is not easily obtainable in the United Kingdom and it is not as responsive to heat as the traditional wok. However, some are slightly flattened at the base and therefore more suitable for electric cookers, and you can use soap and water as often as you want without having to re-season. (If you want to use a common or garden wok on an electric cooker you can buy a ring on which it will sit perfectly.)

The non-stick wok does not need seasoning, nor is it affected by soap. However, as with most non-stick pans, metal utensils and metal pot scourers should not be used. Once the non-stick surface has been scratched it is practically useless, and the utensil reverts to being a traditional wok.

The electric wok is the latest and most hi-tech of the woks. Most have a non-stick surface. It is virtually a portable kitchen, being a combination of cooker and saucepan, and can also be used as a serving dish.

Accessories If you buy your wok at a specialist shop, say a Vietnamese supermarket, instead of at an ordinary supermarket where kits are *de rigueur*, you might consider buying a few accessories at the same time.

To keep the wok steady on a modern cooker you will probably need a wok stand. This is particularly useful if you

LEFT

Above: base and lid of a metal steamer; below: bamboo steamer with lid and ornate wooden cooking chopsticks.

are steaming or deep-frying but it can be dispensed with when stir-frying since everything is happening so quickly and sudden changes of temperature are essential.

A wok brush is a very useful piece of equipment to have in your kitchen. Made from wood or bamboo, it is used to clean the wok after use. The stiffness of the brush works in much the same way as a scourer except that it does not scratch the coating produced by seasoning the wok.

Bamboo steamers are equally useful (buy wood trivets at the same time). The advantage of having bamboo steamers is that they can be stacked one on top of the other and several dishes can be cooked at the same time. They are particularly good for warming up leftovers.

A bamboo strainer, made of a reinforced circle of wire netting with a wooden handle, is handy for lifting ingredients from steam or hot oil, and a wok scoop to toss and turn ingredients when stir-frying seems to work much better than a Western ladle.

You might also like to buy a cleaver. They have wooden handles and come in three weights: light, medium and heavy. They are made of either tempered carbon steel or stainless steel. The former is preferable since it is harder and maintains a sharper cutting edge for a longer time. For Vietnamese cooking it is a case of the sharper the better. Contrary to what people tend to believe, sharper knives are much safer than dull ones, which slip and slide and demand much more effort.

To use a cleaver, you will need a chopping block. The Vietnamese prefer wooden chopping blocks made from the cross-sections of hardwood tree trunks about 38cm/15in in diameter and 15cm/6in thick. They are not easy to obtain, so if you know a good lumber yard ask an attendant to saw you a section from a hardwood tree. Otherwise, get a thick wooden block from a DIY shop or a department store. If all else fails, get the thickest possible plastic cutting board.

If you have managed to get a wooden chopping block, you will need to cure it. To do this, spread 100ml/4fl oz oil over the surface, cover it with aluminium foil and leave it for a couple of days. Then turn the block over and repeat. Once seasoned, you should then wash it with a little soap and water and dry it thoroughly. A wooden chopping block will give you a solid thunk and is heavy enough not to slip and slide and cause accidents. Properly treated, it will last you for the rest of your life.

RIGHT
Top: metal ladle. Left to right: bamboo sieve, basket ladle; wok scoop; glazing brush; larger wok scoop; whisk.

LEFT
Cleavers can be used for chopping practically everything, once you know the technique. To use the cleaver, grasp the handle firmly with your index finger resting on one side of the blade and your thumb pressing against that finger on the other side.

Using the cleaver

Before you put your kitchen to work, you should know two more things. The first is how to sharpen your cleaver. You will need a small abrasive stone with a rough and a smooth honing surface. The rough is used for dull and nicked edges while the smooth is used for keeping good cleavers in perfect condition.

Begin by rinsing and drying the cleaver, then sprinkle a few drops of oil or water on the rough side of the stone. Hold the cleaver with the sharp edge away from you and the blade almost flat, then rub it on the stone by pressing the fingers of the left hand (for right-handed people) lightly on the top surface. Rub it back and forth several times without lifting it, then turn it over and repeat. Rinse the cleaver to remove any stray metal particles then rub it on the smooth surface of the stone a few times to polish the blade.

The second thing you need to know is how to hold the cleaver. There are three ways to do this and all serve different functions. To chop, you need to curl your fingers around the handle with your thumb on the side of the blade. Chop with decisive strokes, using your entire arm and not just your wrist. Firm, decisive chopping means no splintering of bones.

To mince meat, a common technique in Vietnamese cooking, you need to hold the cleaver with your fingers and thumb curled around the handle. The tip of the cutting edge is used as a fulcrum and the blade lifted and dropped, the weight of the cleaver doing all the work. Mincing is very quick; it is even quicker if you use two cleavers, working them up and down alternately, but this requires some practice.

Finally, the cutting grip. Hold the cleaver as for chopping but instead of curling your index finger around the handle, press it against the blade. With your thumb pressing on the other side of the blade, you have maximum control. This way, you can tilt and turn the blade every which way. In Vietnamese cooking, all food is cut into uniformly small pieces. The reason for this is simple: small pieces cook quickly without losing their crunchiness, and if they are the same size they will be uniformly crunchy. It also means that they absorb the taste of the oil and seasonings much more efficiently in spite of the short cooking time.

Techniques

Vietnamese cooking insists on ingredients retaining their natural shape – for example, cauliflower and broccoli are cut into florets. Other vegetables are sliced, shredded, diced or roll cut, depending on the method of cooking. For stir-frying, vegetables are cut as thinly as possible, even shredded, while for braising they are cut into larger pieces. The theory behind this advanced culinary technology is that you have much more surface to be exposed to a quick blast of heat for the one type of cooking and less surface for longer cooking, thereby sealing in and retaining the flavours.

In Vietnamese cooking, cuts are rather different from what you may be accustomed to, but there is a perfectly rational explanation. For instance, to chop poultry, you disjoint the wings first. There is a trick to doing it briskly and effectively: there always is. Snap them back, expose the connecting bone and cut through. The same goes for the legs and thighs. Wings are normally chopped crossways into three pieces, while a leg and thigh would be chopped into five, leaving the major joints – where the upper wing meets the lower and the thigh meats the drumstick – intact. Part of the reason for this is that Orientals are fond of the crunchy cartilage found there. A second advantage is that reassembly is much easier and the finished product looks a lot better.

The bird is then put on its side and with one or more judicious whacks the backbone and breast are separated. The breast is then placed bones down, chopped lengthways and separated. Each half is then cut crossways in three pieces. The back is cut in a similar fashion. To reassemble, follow the exactly opposite procedure – in other words, lay down the backbone first, then the breast and finally the thighs, drumsticks and wings.

The Vietnamese also use the cleaver for mincing, and once you get accustomed to it, you too will come to the inescapable conclusion that there is a difference in taste between meat that goes through a machine and that which

Preparing Poultry

1
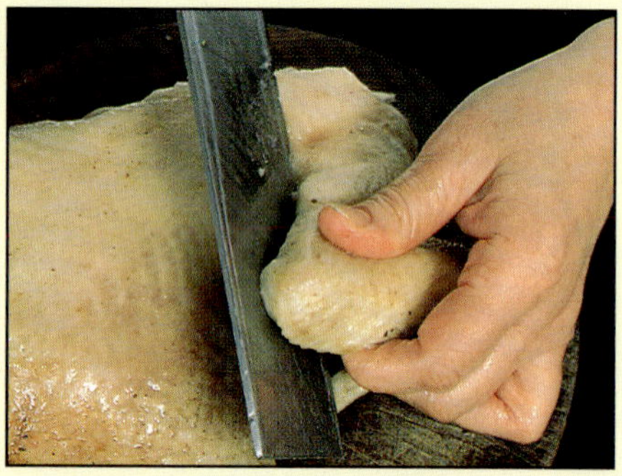

3
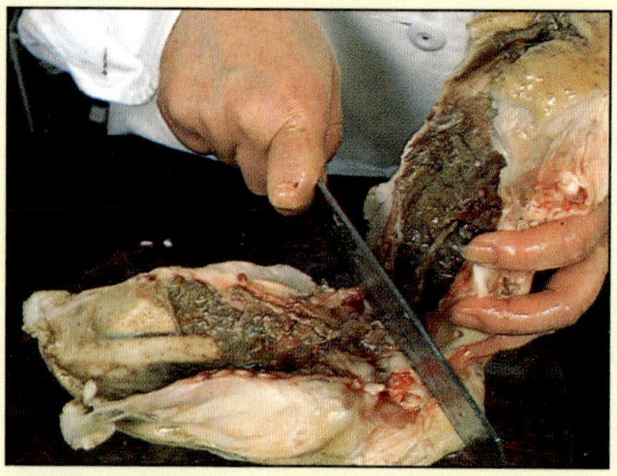

2
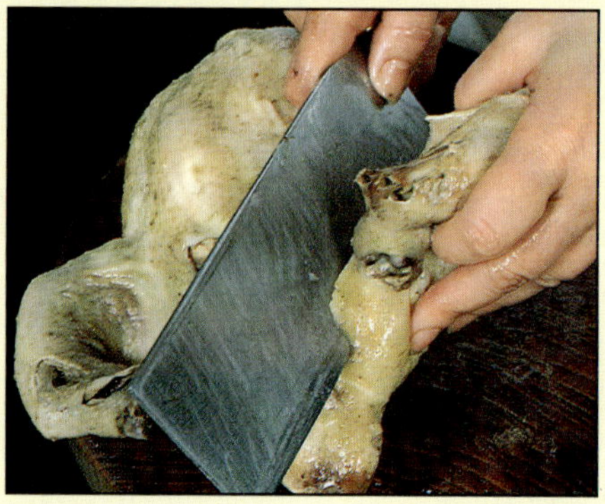

4

1 Pull the wing gently from the body and cut through the joint where it attaches to the body.

2 Similarly, pull the thigh and leg away from the body and cut down through the thigh joint.

3 Holding the body with the tail end upright, carefully and firmly cut down through the backbone.

4 Cut the boned breast sections across into pieces.

you do yourself. That comment applies equally to vegetables.

To mince meat, poultry or seafood, cut them into coarse pieces and then pile the pieces up. Mince by using the tip of the wet cleaver as a fulcrum and saw away; alternatively, chop firmly and swiftly down using a short action. Chop from one end of the pile to the other then chop again, this time at an angle of 90°. Repeat this several times, then slip the cleaver under the food, flip it over and repeat the mincing. (You may find holding the blunt end of the cleaver with the left hand and working the handle up and down with the right easier.) Continue doing this until there is an even consistency.

When slicing, you should hold the food with your fingertips tucked well out of the way, your knuckles forward to act as a guide. You should also avoid lifting the blade higher than your knuckles. The blade should be about 5 mm/⅛ in from the edge of the food and you should slice straight downwards. The thickness is regulated by moving the fingers further away from the edge being cut.

Slicing thinly is paramount for Vietnamese cooking because so much of it is stir-fried. Meat can be cut into thin slices, matchstick strips or cubes; beef should be cut across the grain at a thickness of about 5 mm/⅛ in. Stack the slices up and cut them into narrow slivers and you have matchstick strips – ideal for stir-frying as well as steaming.

Putting meat in the refrigerator for a couple of hours before cutting firms it up and makes it easier to cut neatly (Vietnamese cooking does demand a degree of aesthetics not required of other cuisines).

To cut vegetables diagonally, the food should be held from the top with your fingers slanted across at an angle of 60°. Again, using your knuckles as a guide, slice downwards. Cutting diagonally gives you more cooking surface and is particularly good for stir-frying. For braising, first make a diagonal cut and then turn the vegetable 90° and cut again. In this way you finish up with chunks that will seal in their own flavour.

Cutting, Slicing and Shredding Poultry

1
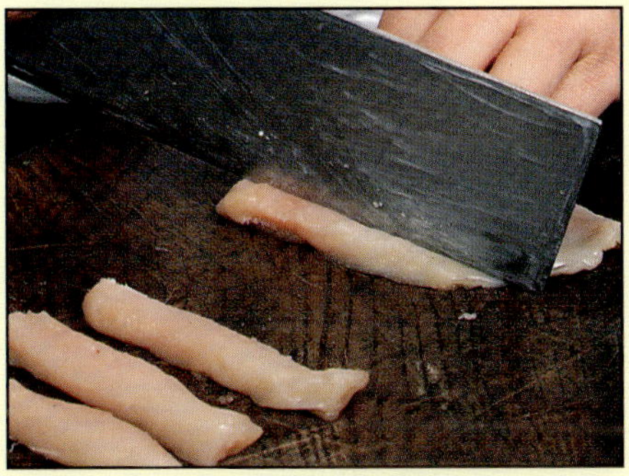

3
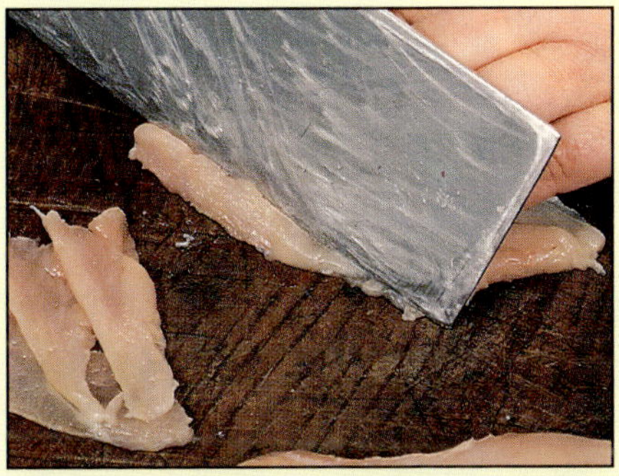

2

4
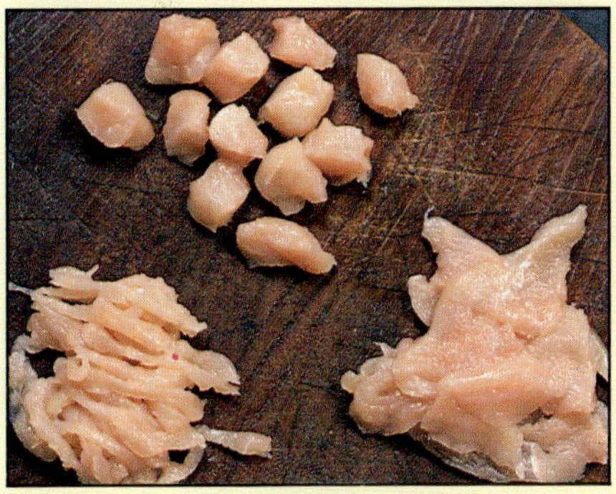

1 Guarding and guiding with one hand, cut the chicken breast lengthways into strips or more thinly into slivers.

2 Cut the strips across into cubes or more finely into diced pieces.

3 Alternatively, hold the cleaver blade at an angle to cut the breast lengthways into thin slices.

4 Top: cubed; Bottom; shreds; thin slices.

Preparing Meat

1

3

2

4

1 Cutting across the grain while guarding and guiding with the other hand, cut the beef into slices.

2 Lay each slice flat and cut the meat into double-size matchstick shreds.

3 Cut shredded meat into small pieces, then chop the pieces finely, repeatedly gathering them into a pile and turning them over as you chop.

4 Top: slices; chopped. Bottom: shreds.

Garnishes

The Vietnamese have an intense dislike of using anything that does not have more than one purpose. The ubiquitous spring onion, for example, is never used simply for seasoning but as a garnish as well. You'd be surprised at how many ways there are of cutting spring onions. They can be cut crossways in the traditional Western way in rounds, diagonally, in lengths or in threads; alternatively, they can be made into brushes. To do this, trim the white ends of the spring onions into 5cm/2in lengths. Using the sharp tip of the cleaver, cut them several times longitudinally from both ends, leaving the middle intact. Place them in a bowl of cold water or water with a couple of ice cubes and put in the refrigerator for several hours. This will curl the ends, giving you the brushes.

The carrot is one of the favourite decorative vegetables of Vietnamese cuisine. I have often watched my father carve the humble carrot into an absolutely amazing number of shapes, too numerous to mention in an introduction to

RIGHT

These carrot roses are quite difficult to make, but are well worth the effort. You can deep freeze them for use at a later date, too.

the food of Vietnam. I have seen birds carved out of a good-sized carrot, as well as tiny, delicate flowers. An example of a less difficult one might give you an idea.

To make carrot roses, you will need a carrot about 5cm/2in in diameter. Wash and peel it, cut out a chunk about 5cm/2in thick and place it on a table. Smooth the edges of this chunk to form the shape of a ball, then cut a cross on its top with a knife so that you have four sectors of equal size. Use a sharp knife to cut a petal about 5mm/⅛in thick on each of the four sides, stopping about 8mm/¼in from the bottom. Cut around the inside of the first layer of petals to form a groove. Cut a second layer of four petals, positioning them so that the centres of the petals are where those of the first layer end, rather like brickwork. Continue until you can no longer carve petals. Soak the carrot in water until ready to use.

LEFT
Garnishes. Attractive presentation of food is very important to the Vietnamese, and a dish's appearance is given as much consideration as the freshness of the ingredients used in it. Decoratively sliced vegetables are chosen for their colours and flavours to complement the dishes they garnish.

OPPOSITE
A family at play, eating rice cakes.

Alternatively, you can peel and cut a carrot into nine discs about 3mm/ 1/10in thick. Make a radial cut on each carrot slice and soak the carrot slices in salted water for 2–3 minutes to soften them. Dry them and pile three small slices together with the cut sides overlapping to make a cone. Stick a toothpick in the centre and use that as a pistil. Pile the slices around the pistil to form a rose.

You can make chilli flowers by slicing chillies in half from the tip to about 1cm/ 1/2in from the bottom. Cut each half into three to give you six petals and separate them from the pistil with a knife. Cut small slants along the edges of each petal and leave the chillies in cold water for at least 2 hours, after which the petals will curl outwards to form a flower.

You may wish to do your carving with something less aggressively macho (do *not* rub your eyes with your fingers after makinga chilli flower) such as a cucumber. Clean and dry the cucumber and slice it evenly down its length. Take one half and slice off the two ends at an angle. Using a small knife, make six very thin slashes, stopping about 8mm/ 1/4in from the other side. Cut through the cucumber at the seventh slash. Curl back every alternate slice and tuck them in firmly so that you have three straight pieces and three curls. Make as many cucumber curls as you like – they brighten up a dish no end.

To make orange wheels, you need a couple of oranges. Begin by making a cross on each side of the first orange. Using this cross as a guide, gouge three narrow strips per quarter. Gouge out the centre of every strip so that you have 16 in all. Cut the orange lengthways in half and cut these halves into slices about 5mm/ 1/8in thick. Repeat with the second and set aside. Onions, radishes, tomatoes and the like can be carved in much the same way.

What to Eat When

Vietnamese breakfasts show the influence of both French and Chinese eating habits. For example, the Vietnamese frequently start the day with a bowl of soup or a meal that looks more like a dinner, as the Chinese do. Other people prefer a bowl of coffee and a croissant or a "French bread" sandwich of cheese, roast chicken or ham. Indeed, I am informed with no small amount of pride that this is becoming more and more commonplace.

Another hot meal is served for lunch, normally taken between noon and 2pm. It is often centred on potage, a clear soup containing either meat or shrimp and vegetables. Rice, stir-fried vegetables and a seafood or meat dish accompany it. As in China, all the dishes are placed on the table at the same time, the family helping themselves to the potage between mouthfuls of food.

Dinner is substantially the same sort of meal as lunch, although on a rather more elaborate and substantial scale. Most Vietnamese would expect to see a bowl of soup, rice, a vegetable stir-fry and at least two dishes of meat, chicken, duck, pork or fish. To finish off, there is fresh fruit – most common are watermelons, mangoes, durians, logans, lychees, jack fruit, star fruit and oranges. Like the Chinese, the Vietnamese rarely eat after meals; most sweets are bought as snacks from pavement vendors.

The Vietnamese eat off a low table called a divan, not dissimilar to a coffee table. Men sit with their legs crossed, while women tuck their legs to one side. A simple straw mat is laid and each person has a bowl with a pair of chopsticks to the right. A bottle of Nuoc Mam sauce is mandatory in much the same way as a bottle of tomato ketchup on American tables.

The food arrives in large bowls brought in by the women, the rice bowl going to the lady of the house who serves everyone else. Her chore completed, everyone helps themselves to small portions of whatever they fancy, a little at a time. Unlike Westerners, the Vietnamese do not heap their bowls with their full meal but prefer to taste each dish on its own merit, rice being the equivalent of a mouthwash between courses. Soup is spooned up at will and can be thought of as the equivalent of wine rather than as a starter.

GLOSSARY

The various influences on Vietnamese cooking have led to the inclusion of a huge variety of ingredients, and some of the more unusual, or those most often used, are described here. They can be found in Oriental stores and, indeed, many are now common-place on supermarket shelves.

Bamboo shoots are sold in cans and should be eaten as soon as possible after opening the can. They will, however, last for up to 6 days in a refrigerator if the water in which they are stored is changed daily. Only about 10 species of bamboo have shoots that are edible.

Banh Pho are short, flat, white Vietnamese rice stick noodles about 4mm/⅛in wide. They cook in minutes in boiling water or soup and should not be overdone. They are used in soup-noodle dishes, particularly the Hanoi soup that goes by the common name of pho.

Banh Trang is the Vietnamese equivalent of ravioli skins. It is round, semi-transparent, thin, hard and dry rice-paper and is used as the wrapping on Vietnamese spring rolls and grilled meats, with salad and herbs. It is made from a dough of finely ground rice, water and salt, with tapioca (cassava) flour as a binding agent.

The dough is passed through rollers and then cut into circles 16–34cm/7–14in in diameter. These are then put on bamboo mats to dry in the sun. Once dry, they will keep indefinitely. To use, they must be moistened by covering with a damp cloth until soft or by dipping quickly into warm water. To get a crisp, golden-brown colour, the wrappers can be brushed lightly with a sugar-water solution before frying.

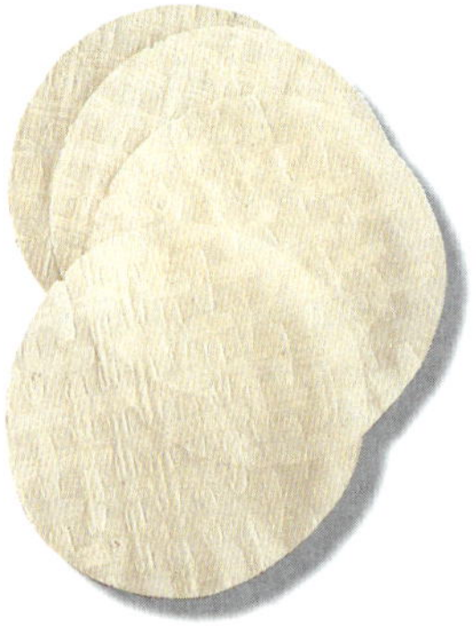

Bean curd is made from dried soya beans, soaked, puréed and boiled with water. The resulting milky liquid is strained and then mixed with a coagulant or natural solidifier which causes it to form curds. These are then taken to wooden tubs lined with cloth and pressed until they form bean curd.

The bean curd is then cut into small squares and stored in cold water. Fresh bean curd is inexpensive and easily available. Although it is bland, it absorbs the flavours in which it is cooked. It was discovered during the Han Dynasty by a group of researchers who were assigned to investigate new medicines. Their result was bean curd, which became known as "meat without bones".

Bean thread vermicelli are noodles resembling strands of clear plastic and are also called "transparent" or "cellophane" vermicelli. Cooked as noodles, they are used in soups, braised dishes and hotpots. In Szechwan and neighbouring Tibet, they are first softened in water and then stir-fried with vegetables. In Indonesia, Malaysia and Singapore, the boiled noodles are added to sweet drinks and desserts together with palm sugar syrup, coconut milk and diced vegetables such as yam or sweet potato, or sweet corn kernels.

Black beans invariably mean fermented black beans, the original shih or darkened, salted soya beans of China. Dried soya beans are cooked, salted and fermented until they become almost black and soft. They can be kept almost indefinitely in airtight jars. They should be washed and dried before use and may be cooked whole, finely chopped or mashed.

Black vinegar is a dark, mild, almost sweet vinegar that has only one equivalent: balsamic vinegar. It is usually made from glutinous rice or sorghum which gives it its distinctive taste. The better varieties have a range of flavours, from smoky to wine-yeasty. In central China and some parts of the north, black vinegar is used like tomato ketchup and is added to almost every dish.

Chillies exist in many variations, varying in size and shape as well as colour and intensity of flavour. Generally, green chillies are milder than the red ones, and deseeding them reduces their intensity.

Whole, fresh chillies may be added directly to dishes or may be chopped and shredded into curries, soups and stir-fries, or mixed with soya sauce, vinegar or fish sauce to be used as dips. They may be dried or steeped in oil to make a clear, hot-flavoured oil. which is used extensively in China.

Chinese mushrooms is the common name for the dried black (or rather pale buff or brown) mushrooms. The best are lighter coloured with plump caps, but they are very expensive. Long ago the Chinese learned that drying the mushrooms intensifies their flavour.

They should be soaked in warm water for about 20 minutes, then squeezed to get rid of the salt. The stalks should be cut off as they are too tough to eat. They are particularly good when they are simmered gently in a light broth with soya sauce and rice wine.

Chinese stem ginger is probably better known as ginger preserve. The Chinese normally preserve it with cucumber, fruits and spices. It is used as a relish and in sweet-and-sour sauces.

Coconut milk was originally made by painstakingly grating the kernel and mixing it with a little water. The resulting mixture then had to be squeezed through a piece of cloth. Today with the advent of the liquidizer, the kernel is ground together with a little water and the mixture squeezed by hand, a much faster process. The first squeeze produces the best milk and is called coconut cream. After a second squeeze, the dry fibre pulp is thrown away. There are a number of excellent brands of canned coconut milk available, but it should be remembered that it will keep for only a few hours at room temperature, or two days in a refrigerator. If there is a great deal left over, it should be frozen. A third way of making coconut milk is to soak desiccated coconut in hot water or milk and squeeze this through a piece of cloth in the traditional manner. The first squeeze is very rich and tends to curdle during cooking. To avoid this, continual stirring is recommended.

Coriander leaves are used extensively in Southeast Asian cooking although they are hardly used in Japan. The flavour is fresh, strong, earthy and something of an acquired taste.

Coriander roots are used particularly in Thailand where they are ground together with the stems for curry pastes and sauces. There the leaves are used in salads and as a garnish.

Cumin is Mediterranean in origin and has travelled east – unlike spaghetti. It is both pungent and aromatic. The seeds should be roasted in a dry pan or in a very hot oven before using, either whole or ground. The temperature should be high enough to make them pop.

Dried jellyfish has little taste but is valued for its crunchy texture. It is the salted and sun-dried skin of the mantle of the jellyfish and said by Westerners to be as tasy as a rubber band. It should be soaked in warm water for several hours and does not require cooking, which only serves to toughen it. It is usually shredded finely and marinated in vinegar to be served in a salad. Add a little sesame oil and it is transformed into the most delicious and crunchy salad.

Five-spice powder is an aromatic, Chinese spice powder, made according to an ancient formula using three native spices – star anise, cassia bark and Szechwan peppercorns – with the seeds of wild fennel and cloves from the nearby Moluccas or Spice Islands.

The five spices in their whole form can be used as an oriental bouquet garni, tied up in a small cheesecloth bag and put into stews and the like and retrieved before serving. Five-spice powder can also be made into a dip by adding five-spice powder to heated salt.

You can make your own five-spice powder by placing 40 Szechwan peppercorns, 2 cinnamon sticks 5cm/2in long, 1½ tsp fennel seeds, 12 whole cloves and 2 whole star anise in a mortar or spice grinder and grind to a fine powder. This should produce about 25g/1oz five-spice powder. Store in a tightly closed jar. It will keep for about three months.

To make five-spice salt, heat a wok or pan over medium heat. Pour in 50g/2oz salt and heat through, stirring continuously, until well heated. Cool briefly before stirring in the five-spice powder. When cool, the mixture can be stored in a spice jar. It can be used as a dip for roasted, grilled and fried meats, or sprinkled over food as a seasoning prior to deep-frying.

Galangal (greater and lesser species) is a member of the ginger family and, in many countries, is used as a substitute. It has a hot, peppery taste and is used mainly as a flavouring. In Thailand, greater galangal is ground with chillies and other herbs and spices to make a refreshing drink. Lesser galangal is eaten as a vegetable, both raw and cooked. In Indonesia lesser galangal is used as a spice.

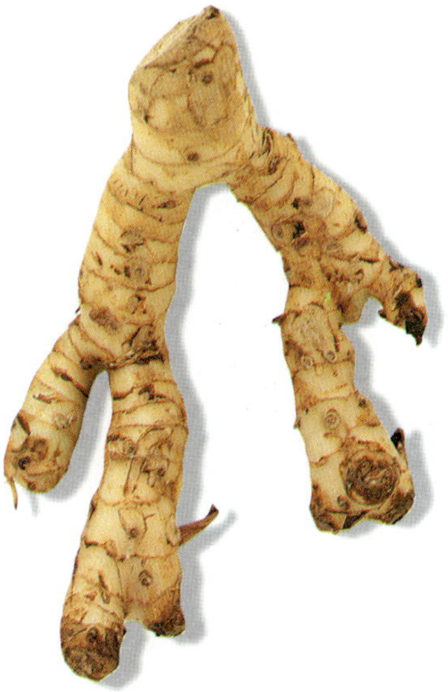

Ground chillies are made from dried pods, which are also used whole, broken or desiccated. They are best dried by roasting in a hot oven or in a dry pan. They are then ground to a coarse powder which is then added to ground rice. This mixture is used as a strongly flavoured thickener or coating for fried foods. It may also be sprinkled over foods as a condiment.

Ground coriander is one of the essential ingredients in curry powders. It is made from the seed spice and it is best to buy the seed spice whole and grind it when needed. To get the best out of the coriander seed, it is advisable to toast first in an oven and then grind it finely.

Hoisin sauce is the barbeque sauce of Southeast Asia. Made from red rice which is coloured with a natural food dye, usually annatto seeds, it is a sweet-tasting, thick, reddish-brown sauce best used as a condiment for roast pork and poultry.

It is made from fermented soya bean paste, sugar, garlic and spices, normally five-spice. Hoisin sauce should not be confused with the Chinese barbeque sauce, sha cha jiang.

Lemon grass has been used in this country and in Europe for centuries under the better known name citronella, named for its distinct lemon scent and flavour. It is best used fresh, but can be kept, loosely wrapped, in the refrigerator for about a week and a half. To store, the bulb end should be rinsed and dried, then finely sliced or chopped. When ready for use, it should be slit open lengthways to release the flavour.

Noodles are one of the mainstays in the Asian diet and were the inspiration for spaghetti. They are used extensively in Vietnam where they are enjoyed, in some form, at every meal.

Dried noodles should be kept in an airtight container where they will last for several months. They are usually cooked by boiling in salted water, like pasta.

Nuoc Mam (or fish) sauce is a powerfully flavoured, pungent seasoning sauce. It is used extensively in Southeast Asia, particularly Burma, Cambodia, Thailand and Vietnam. It is made by layering fish and salt into large barrels and allowing the fish to ferment for three or more months before the accumulated liquid is siphoned off, filtered and bottled.

In Vietnam Nuoc Mam is made into different dipping sauces by adding chillies, ground, roasted peanuts, sugar and other ingredients. It is very much an acquired taste, and substitutes such as soya sauce are sufficiently exotic.

Oyster sauce is one of the most popular bottled sauces in Southeast Asia. Made from dried oysters, it is thick and richly flavoured. The cheaper brands tend to be more salty. The original sauce was much thinner and contained fragments of fermented, dried oysters. Many people use it as a superior version of soya sauce, but Asians use it as an accompaniment for stir-fried vegetables and to flavour and colour braised and stir-fried dishes.

Paprika is also known as capsicum or bell peppers. In Vietnam it is used as a vegetable and as a spice. In its latter guise, it is dried and ground to a powder.

Pomelo is a large Chinese fruit that resembles a grapefruit. It tapers slightly at the stem end and has a thick, sweet, slightly rough-textured skin and a dry, semi-sweet flesh. Like many other fruits, it is sometimes eaten in Southeast Asia with salt.

Rice vermicelli is a fine, extruded, creamy-coloured noodle, made from a dough of finely ground rice and water. It cooks almost instantly, needing only to be dipped in very hot water and drained thoroughly.

Rice vermicelli can be stir-fried and served as soft noodles. It should be softened first and drained before stir-frying. To deep-fry, the dried noodles are added directly to the oil.

Sake is made by introducing a yeast mould into steamed rice to begin the fermentation process. Later lactic acid is added to prevent contamination. The milky fermentation is then filtered and, about 45 days later, results in a crystal clear liquid – sake.

The word itself is the name for Japan's most popular beverage and all Japanese alcoholic drinks. Connoisseurs advise that it be drunk immediately and, once the bottle is opened, it should be finished the same day. In any event, sake should not be left undrunk for more than a year.

Saltfish (or salted cod) was first imported from Newfoundland in Canada as survival food for the natives of British colonies. Just how it found its way to Vietnam is not clear but it has become something of a delicacy of not only Southeast Asia but the West Indies and Africa as well. It can be bought in most ethnic foodshops.

Soya sauce is made from fermented soya beans mixed with a roasted grain, normally wheat. It is injected with a yeast mould and after fermentation begins, salt is added. Yeast is added for further fermentation and the liquid is left in vats for several months and then filtered.

Light soya sauce is thin, salty and light in flavour and is used as a condiment and in cooking where its light colour will not spoil the colours of the ingredients, particularly seafood.

Dark soya sauce is thicker with a full-bodied flavour and is used to add colour where needed. Generally it is less salty than the light soya sauce. The Chinese mushroom soya sauce is made with the addition of flavourings from Chinese straw mushrooms.

Lu Soy is a "master sauce" made from soya sauce with sugar, ginger and five-spice and is used for simmering poultry and other meats that benefit from a rich flavour and a dark colour.

Sweet soya sauce is a dark, sweet sauce made with soya sauce, sugar and malt sugar. It has a distinctive malty taste, which makes it ideal as a dip for fried snacks, poultry and seafood.

Star anise is the seed pods of one of the Magnolia trees. The tan-coloured, eight-pointed pods resemble stars, hence the name. When dried, a shiny, flat, light brown seed is revealed in each point. It has a pronounced licorice flavour and the ground spice is one of the essential ingredients in the Chinese five-spice powder. In Vietnam it is used primarily in simmered dishes and for making stock.

Straw mushrooms are grown on paddy-straw, left over from harvested wheat, which gives them a distinctly earthy taste. Generally, they are packed in water and canned. They are globe-shaped, about the size of quail's eggs, and buff-coloured, growing grey-black as they become older. They have no stems but a cross-section reveals an internal stem.

Sugar cane is reasonably easy to obtain from large greengrocers, West Indian shops and some markets that specialize in foreign produce. It is cultivated exclusively for its sweet sap that is made into sugar.

The sugar cane bought for cooking consists of the stem, the leaves being chopped off in the cane fields. The cane should be very carefully peeled with a strong, sharp knife.

Szechwan peppercorns are aromatic, small, red-brown seeds from the prickly ash tree known as fagara. The whole "peppercorns" can be kept for years without loss of flavour if stored in a tightly sealed jar away from light, heat and moisture. In China, they are mixed into heated fine salt to produce pepper-salt, a fragrant, salty dip for grilled and fried foods and often used in marinades.

Turmeric, a native of Southeast Asia, belongs to the same family as ginger and galangal. It has a bright orange-yellow flesh with a strong, earthy smell and a slightly bitter taste. The flesh is responsible for the yellow colour we associate with curry powders and it overpowers all other spices.

Dried turmeric is best stored in a tightly sealed jar and used with discretion. Because of its colour, it is an effective substitute for saffron. Like many spices in the East, it is credited with medicinal qualities and is taken both internally and externally.

Wood ear fungus is known under a variety of names. Perhaps the most common is derived from its habitat of decayed wood. The Chinese call it cloud ears because it resembles the clouds rendered with a paint brush in a Chinese painting. It is also called Judas or Jew's ear from its botanical name *(Auricularia auriculajudae)* or perhaps some other inspiration, and the Thai translation is rat's ear.

It is valued for its subtle, delicate flavour and slightly crunchy "bite". It is always sold in its dried form and looks like a curly seaweed. When soaked, it expands to five times its dried size, so a little goes a long way. It should be rinsed thoroughly to wash out the grains of sand that seem to cling to it. It does not require long cooking and has no flavour of its own but readily absorbs seasonings. It does not like moisture and should be stored in a sealed container in a cool, dry place.

Yellow bean sauce is made according to the ancient recipe for jiang or pickled yellow soya beans in a salty liquid. It is normally bought in cans and jars but it is best transferred to a jar in which it can be stored in a refrigerator almost indefinitely.

BACK TO BASICS

Throughout this book reference is made to the stock needed to form the "gravy" of many of the dishes. This should be light and not swamp the other ingredients. My father used to spend endless hours preparing the stock and he always said that the secret of a good pho was in the stock. On the back hole of our cast-iron Chinese cooker he always had a stock pot ready to boil up at a minute's notice, religiously attending to it daily.

Today, when time is at a premium, it is difficult to maintain this tradition. However, stock can be kept in a freezer, and of course there is always the ubiquitous bouillon cube – use a good-quality one. A lot of supermarkets sell canned stock for soups, and in large Asian stores you will find cans of stock for various traditional soups which are very useful. The hot and sour stock is one I would recommend.

Brown Stock

MAKES ABOUT 2.8 LITRES/5 PINTS

- **1 onion, cut into quarters**
- **3 celery sticks, chopped (use the heart and top as well)**
- **2 cloves**
- **1 clove garlic**
- **4 peppercorns**
- **1 cm/½ in piece unpeeled root ginger**
- **3.4 litres/6 pt cold water**

1 Place all the ingredients in a large pot with a well-fitting lid and bring to the boil. Adjust the heat to maintain a faint simmer. (It is important to make sure that the stock is not boiled as boiling results in a cloudy broth.) Simmer for 4–5 hours, stirring occasionally.

2 Leave to cool, then strain. Use as required.

Vegetable Stock

MAKES 1.7 LITRES/3 PINTS

- **4 carrots, roughly chopped**
- **4 celery sticks, preferably the heart, tops and leaves, roughly chopped**
- **3 potatoes, peeled and quartered**
- **3 spring onions, roughly cut**
- **4 pieces wood ear fungus, soaked and drained**
- **4 peppercorns**
- **2 cloves**
- **2.2 litres/4pt cold water**

1 Bring all the ingredients to the boil in a heavy pan. Immediately reduce the heat, and then adjust to simmer for 3 hours. Use as required.

◀ *Drying grain or cassava on hot corrugated roof tops is a common practice.*

Chicken Stock

MAKES ABOUT 2.8 LITRES/5 PINTS

The carcass of the Sunday joint is ideal; thighs, wings and feet also make good stock. After 30 minutes, remove any meat to use in a dish and carry on simmering the bones to give a flavoursome broth.

- **1.5–1.75kg/3–4lb chicken bones**
- **1cm/½in root ginger, peeled and sliced**
- **2 spring onions, cut into halves**
- **4 peppercorns**
- **3.4 litres/6pt cold water**

1 Place all the ingredients in a heavy pan with a well-fitting lid. Bring to the boil, then immediately reduce the heat to a gentle simmer. Skim off the grey foam until clear.

2 Bring to the boil again, reducing the heat the moment the first bubbles appear. Adjust the heat until the stock is just simmering. Cover and leave for 3–4 hours.

3 Leave to cool, then strain and use as required.

Fish Stock

MAKES 0.8 LITRE/1½ PINTS

Use any pieces of fish bits, heads and all.

- **800g/2lb fish bits**
- **1 onion, roughly cut**
- **1 carrot, roughly cut**
- **2 stalks celery, roughly cut**
- **1 clove garlic**
- **4 black peppercorns**
- **1.1 litre/2pt water**

1 Place all the ingredients in a heavy pan with a tight-fitting lid, and bring to the boil. Reduce the heat immediately, and skim off any grey foam that appears until a clear broth is left. Adjust the heat and leave to simmer for about 3 hours. Use as required.

SOUPS AND STARTERS

Prawns with Sesame Seeds on Toast

CHAO TÔM VOI ME

SERVES 4

- **4 tbsp white sesame seeds**
- **½ tbsp dried prawns (optional)**
- **175g/6oz peeled prawns, finely chopped**
- **2 cloves garlic, crushed and chopped**
- **½ tsp fresh root ginger, grated**
- **1 small onion, grated**
- **1 small egg, beaten**
- **salt and black pepper**
- **cornflour for dusting**
- **1 thin French stick or 8 slices bread, crusts cut off**
- **vegetable oil for deep-frying**

1 Toast the sesame seeds in a dry pan until they begin to brown, shaking frequently to prevent them from burning.

2 If using dried prawns, soak in warm water until soft. Drain thoroughly and squeeze out excess water. Chop them finely. Combine the dried and fresh prawns, garlic, ginger, grated onion, egg, salt and black pepper and knead together with your hands. The mixture should be stiff but not too stiff to spread. If it is too runny, dust with the cornflour.

3 Cut the French bread into 1cm/½in slices or cut the slices of bread into triangles or shape using pastry cutters. Press the sesame seeds firmly into the prawn mixture, using the back of a wooden spoon so that the prawn mixture is also pressed firmly on to the bread. Refrigerate for 2 hours or longer if possible.

4 Heat enough oil to just deep-fry the rounds, prawn side down, for 1 minute. Using a fish slice, turn carefully and fry the other side for a further minute. Drain on absorbent kitchen paper and serve hot.

Beef Pho

PHO BO

SERVES 4

My father used to serve this up on Saturdays or Sundays, depending on what time we all got up. In Vietnam it is sold by street vendors as a breakfast, late-night snack or lunch. To make it more satisfying or to make a change, hard-boiled egg cut into quarters can be added or substituted for the beef.

- **225g/8oz broad rice noodles (Banh Pho) or flat egg noodles**
- **1 onion, peeled and chopped into rings**
- **juice from 1 lemon**
- **4 tbsp fresh coriander, finely chopped**
- **4 lettuce leaves, washed and finely shredded**
- **4 tbsp fresh mint, finely chopped**
- **1 lemon or lime, cut into quarters**
- **Beef stock (or use a good-quality bouillon cube)**
- **100g/4oz raw rump steak, thinly shredded**
- **3 or 4 fresh hot red or green chilli peppers, cut into rings (optional)**
- **90ml/6 tbsp Nuoc Mam sauce or 60ml/4 tbsp Maggi liquid seasoning mixed with 30ml/2 tbsp lemon juice, 1 clove garlic, diced, and ½ spring onion, thinly chopped**

1 Soak the noodles for 30 minutes in warm water, until just soft. Drain and keep warm. Soak the onion rings in the lemon juice for 20 minutes.

2 Arrange the coriander, mint, lettuce and lemon or lime wedges on different plates and place on the table.

3 Heat up the prepared stock to boiling point and put the sliced beef, the noodles and warmed soup bowls on the table.

4 First add the noodles to the soup bowls, then follow with the lettuce and herbs then the onion and chillies if desired. Add the meat, placing it in a single layer over the whole. Pour the boiling stock over the paper-thin meat, turning it from raw to rare and releasing the scents and flavours of the coriander, mint and chilli. Add the Nuoc Mam sauce, a squeeze of the lemon or lime and slurp away.

Prawn Pho

PHO TÔM

SERVES 4

Prawn Pho is a very light soup. It is simple yet delicious and unusual as prawns are used in a broth. As a variation, and to make it a little more substantial, I have often added prawn balls. These are simple to make.

- **2 pieces black wood ear fungus or 8 button mushrooms**
- **850ml/1½ pt fish stock (page 23, or use a good-quality vegetable, fish or chicken stock cube)**
- **2 cucumber, peeled**
- **175g/6oz bean thread vermicelli or spaghetti**
- **225g/8oz fresh prawns, cooked and peeled**
- **150ml/¼ pt Nuoc Mam sauce or 60ml/4 tbsp Maggi liquid seasoning mixed with 30ml/2 tbsp lemon juice, 2 crushed anchovies or 8ml/½ tbsp anchovy essence, 1 garlic clove, diced, and ¼ spring onion, finely chopped**
- **4 large, cooked, unpeeled prawns, to garnish**

1 Soak the black wood ear fungus for 10 minutes or until soft in nearly boiling water. When soft, slice thinly and place in stock. Add the button mushrooms to the stock if using those instead. Put into a dish and place on the table.

2 Slice the cucumber into thin rounds or cut into fine matchsticks. Place in a dish and put on the table.

3 Soak the vermicelli in water that has been boiled and allowed to cool slightly (above 5 minutes). Drain and place in four bowls.

4 Place the prawns in a bowl and put on the table. Meanwhile boil and simmer the stock.

5 The guests garnish their bowls with the ingredients in the dishes placed on the table, then pour the hot stock over the whole. The Nuoc Mam sauce is added to taste and the soup bowls are garnished with the unpeeled prawns.

Prawn Balls

TÔM HEO VIÊN

SERVES 4

- **175g/6 oz prawns, minced**
- **1 small hard-boiled egg, finely minced**
- **1 small onion, finely minced**
- **1 egg, beaten**
- **salt and pepper**

1 Mix all the ingredients using your hand, then shape into small balls. Drop into the simmering broth to cook.

Chicken Pho

PHO GÀ

SERVES 4

Traditionally, pho is only made with beef. It is a sign of the times, however, that it was recently spotted in Saigon being made with chicken and prawns. My father used to ring the changes by adding a combination of these ingredients and those in the Beef Pho and Prawn Pho recipes. We used to call the soups by numbers. For example, Number 9 soup had 9 ingredients in: broth, noodles, beef, boiled egg, shredded lettuce, sliced onion in lemon juice, spring onions, coriander and mint. We also had the chicken soup when ill – the light wood ear fungi are very nutritious and good for the spirit.

- **3 celery sticks, finely chopped**
- **3 spring onions, chopped into rings (use green tops as well)**
- **275g/10oz cooked chicken, finely shredded**
- **225g/8oz flour sticks or spaghetti noodles**
- **850ml/1½pt chicken stock (page 23, or use good-quality bouillon cube)**
- **2 pieces light wood ear fungus or 8 white button mushrooms, finely sliced**

1 Place the celery and spring onions in a bowl and put on the table. Place the cooked shredded chicken in a separate bowl and put that on the table also.

2 Follow the instructions on the flour sticks pack, or boil up the spaghetti until just soft. Drain and rinse with some boiling water. Place in 4 bowls.

3 Boil up the chicken stock until simmering, then add the light wood ear fungus or the mushrooms. Place in a bowl and put on the table.

4 The guests should put a mixture of celery, spring onion, and shredded chicken onto the noodles then ladle the hot chicken broth into the bowls.

Prawn Crystal Spring Rolls

BÁNH CUỐN TÔM VIỆT NAM

SERVES 4

- ★ **175g/6 oz cooked crispy roast pork or 4 fresh boneless pork streaky rashers**
- ★ **45ml/3 tbsp clear honey**
- ★ **30ml/2 tbsp dry sherry**
- ★ **1 tsp chilli powder**
- ★ **225g/8oz rice vermicelli**
- ★ **450g/1lb fresh prawns, cooked and halved**
- ★ **175g/6oz cooked chicken, finely chopped**
- ★ **3 pickled onions, cut into fine strips**
- ★ **3 pickled gherkins, cut into fine strips**
- ★ **1 carrot, grated**
- ★ **1 packet of round Banh Trang rice paper**

DIPPING SAUCE

- ★ **100ml/4fl oz Nuoc Mam sauce or Maggi liquid seasoning**
- ★ **1 red chilli pepper, finely chopped**
- ★ **1 clove garlic, finely chopped**
- ★ **30–45ml/2–3 tbsp lemon juice**
- ★ **10ml/2 tsp wine vinegar**
- ★ **10ml/2 tsp ginger wine**
- ★ **1 tsp sugar**

TO SERVE

- ★ **1 Webbs or round lettuce**
- ★ **sprigs of coriander**
- ★ **sprigs of mint**

1 To make the cold crispy pork, take the four rashers of fresh boneless pork. Mix the honey, dry sherry and chilli powder thoroughly. Spread the mixture over the pork. Allow to rest for 1 hour or longer if possible.

2 Grill the pork slices until really crisp. Turn often so that they are evenly cooked. Allow to cool and cut into thin strips.

3 Make the dipping sauce by combining all the ingredients and mixing thoroughly.

4 Soak the rice vermicelli in boiled water, slightly cooled. When soft, drain thoroughly and leave to cool.

5 Place a clean tea towel on the surface you are working on. Dip single sheets of Banh Trang into warm water and place on the tea towel. They should be pliable and soft. Place some cold vermicelli, some prawns, chicken, pork, pickled onion, gherkin and carrot near the centre of the Banh Trang but towards the bottom edge. Spread the filling out to a sausage shape. Roll the bottom edge of the Banh Trang up and tuck tightly under the mixture. Fold the left and right sides into the centre and then continue rolling away from you. This roll will be transparent and allow you to see the mixture inside. Continue until the mixture is used up.

6 Place the cold, rolled, transparent spring rolls on a platter. Guests help themselves to lettuce leaves, one at a time. The roll is placed on the leaf and some mint and coriander are added. The whole is rolled up and dipped in the dipping sauce.

A common way of carrying produce to and from market is over the shoulder, in a don ganh.

Fish Crystal Spring Rolls

BÌ GÚÔN CÁ

SERVES 4

- **1 medium-sized fresh red snapper, sea bass or carp, cleaned and gutted**
- **2 tsp salt**
- **45ml/3 tbsp dry sherry**
- **30ml/2 tbsp ginger wine**
- **20g/1¾oz cornflour**
- **vegetable oil**
- **175g/6oz rice vermicelli**
- **2 pickled gherkins, chopped**
- **2 pickled onions, chopped**
- **1 carrot, grated**
- **1 packet round Banh Trang rice paper**

DIPPING SAUCE

- **60ml/4 tbsp Nuoc Mam or Maggi liquid seasoning**
- **1 red chilli pepper, finely chopped**
- **1 clove garlic, finely chopped**
- **15ml/1 tbsp lemon juice**
- **5ml/1 tsp cider vinegar or wine vinegar**
- **1 tsp sugar**
- **10ml/2 tsp dry sherry**

TO SERVE

- **sprigs of coriander**
- **sprigs of mint**
- **1 Webbs or round lettuce**

1 Make slanting slashes down both sides of the fish, about 2cm/¾in apart. Mix the salt, sherry, ginger wine and 15g/½oz cornflour in a dish large enough to contain the fish. Roll the fish in this mixture until well coated and then leave to stand for 30 minutes, turning several times.

2 Remove the fish from the dish and dust with the remaining cornflour. Heat the oil in a pan big enough to hold the fish and fry over moderate heat for about 12 minutes, turning once, very gently. Drain on absorbent kitchen paper. Keep the fish warm as you assemble the other ingredients.

3 Soak the rice vermicelli in warm water until soft. Drain thoroughly.

4 Combine all the ingredients for the dipping sauce and mix thoroughly. Toss the gherkins, onions and carrot into the rice vermicelli.

5 Assemble all the components on the table. The fish should be warm and gently scraped away from the bones. Provide two bowls of warm water for dipping the Banh Trang in. The guests help themselves to a round rice paper. This is dipped into the warm water and removed before it disintegrates. It should be soft and pliable. The fish, rice vermicelli, mint and coriander are placed on the rice paper. It is then rolled up to a pencil shape and placed on a piece of lettuce. A lettuce leaf is then rolled around the spring roll and dipped into the dipping sauce.

Beef Crystal Spring Rolls

BÁNH CUÕN THIT BÒ VIÊT NAM

SERVES 4

MARINADE

- **1 tsp lemon grass, finely minced (if this is unavailable, use the juice of a lemon and its grated rind)**
- **1 tsp garlic, finely minced**
- **15ml/1 tbsp ginger wine**

- **225g/8oz steak, cut against the grain into pieces 3mm/⅛ thick and 5cm/2in long**
- **125g/6oz rice vermicelli**
- **2 pickled onions, finely cut**
- **2 pickled gherkins, finely cut**
- **1 carrot, grated**
- **1 packet round Banh Trang rice paper**
- **warmed water in a bowl on the table**

DIPPING SAUCE

- **60ml/4 tbsp Nuoc Mam sauce or Maggi liquid seasoning**
- **1 red chilli pepper, finely chopped**
- **1 clove of garlic, finely chopped**
- **15ml/1 tbsp lime or lemon juice**
- **5ml/1 tsp wine vinegar**
- **1 tsp sugar**
- **10ml/2 tsp dry sherry**

TO SERVE

- **1 Webbs or round lettuce**
- **sprigs of coriander**

1 Combine the marinade ingredients together and marinade the beef slices. Leave for 2–3 hours.

2 Soak the rice vermicelli. When soft, drain thoroughly. Toss the cold rice vermicelli, pickled onion, gherkin and carrot together and place on the table in a dish.

3 Prepare the dipping sauce by mixing all dipping ingredients together and stir well. Put the lettuce leaves in a dish, the coriander and mint on a flat plate, and place on the table. Put the Banh Trang on a plate and place on the table.

4 Put warm water in a bowl that is large enough for the Banh Trang to be dipped in on the table. Put either a table-top barbecue or a fondue on the table and bring the marinated meat to the table for the guests to cook. If neither is available, grill the meat very quickly, or fry in a pan with a little vegetable oil. Either way the cooking time is minimal, as thinly cut meat cooks extremely quickly. Excessive cooking toughens the meat.

5 Guests should help themselves by dipping a Banh Trang into the warm water until it becomes soft and pliable. They then place some of the vermicelli and pickle, mint and coriander and the cooked pieces of beef on the Banh Trang. The mixture is then rolled up and placed on a fresh piece of lettuce. The lettuce leaf is rolled around it and then dipped in the sauce.

Beef Crystal Spring Rolls ▶

Vietnamese Spring Rolls

CHA GIÒ VIÊT NAM

SERVES 6

These delicious spring rolls should not be confused with the Chinese pancake rolls. Traditionally, Vietnamese people would serve these at a party or a special occasion. They do take a bit of time to make , but the result is well worth the effort.

- **100g/4oz bean thread vermicelli**
- **2 dried Chinese mushrooms or 4 button mushrooms**
- **2 pieces black wood ear fungus**
- **1 tbsp dried prawns or shrimps or 8 fresh prawns, finely minced**
- **2 cloves garlic, minced**
- **1 carrot, grated**
- **1 onion, grated**
- **100g/4oz pork, minced**
- **15ml/1 tbsp Nuoc Mam sauce or 15ml/1 tbsp light soya sauce with 2 anchovies crushed into it and a dash of lime or lemon juice**
- **black pepper**
- **1 egg, beaten**
- **1 packet of quadrant-shaped or round Banh Trang rice paper**
- **vegetable oil for frying**

DIPPING SAUCE

- **30ml/2 tbsp Nuoc Mam sauce or 30ml/2 tbsp Maggi liquid seasoning**
- **1 clove garlic, finely chopped**
- **1 red chilli pepper, finely chopped**
- **10ml/2 tsp lime or lemon juice**
- **5ml/1 tsp cider vinegar or wine vinegar**
- **1 tsp sugar**

TO SERVE

- **1 Webbs or round lettuce**
- **sprigs of coriander**
- **sprigs of mint**

1 Make the dipping sauce first. Combine all the ingredients in a dish and stir thoroughly.

2 Soak the vermicelli in boiled water slightly cooled until soft and drain thoroughly. Cut with kitchen scissors to make shorter strands.

3 Soak the Chinese mushrooms and black wood ear fungus in boiled water that has cooled slightly. When soft, drain thoroughly, gently squeezing out any excess water. Cut finely. If using button mushrooms, wash, drain and chop finely.

4 Soak the dried prawns or shrimp in boiled water that has cooled slightly until soft and then drain thoroughly. Mince finely. If using fresh prawns, wash, drain and mince.

5 Place the vermicelli, garlic, carrot, onion, black wood ear fungus, mushrooms, dried prawns or shrimps, minced pork, Nuoc Mam sauce, black pepper and egg in a large mixing bowl. With your hands, mix all the ingredients thoroughly until the mixture is stiff enough to be shaped.

6 Place some boiled water that has cooled slightly in a large bowl. Spread a clean tea towel on the surface you are going to roll on. If using the quadrant Banh Trang rice paper, take one piece and dip it into the water. Place it on the tea towel. Take another piece of rice paper and repeat.

The rice paper should turn soft and pliable. (It is very important not to leave the rice paper too long in the water.)

7 Place the second piece of rice paper on the first. The rounded edge of the quadrant should be at the bottom facing you and the second piece placed about 5cm/2in above but overlapping. Place a small amount of the mixture where the pieces overlap at the bottom, on the rounded edge. Form the mixture into a sausage shape.

8 Carefully roll the bottom rounded edge over the mixture, tucking the edge under the mixture. Fold over the left and right sides to the middle, then roll the parcel away from you. Repeat these three steps until all the mixture has been used. Be careful not to pack your rolls with too much mixture and try to roll them as tightly as possible, otherwise they will burst when fried.

9 If using the round rice paper, pass it through the water and place it on the tea towel. Put some mixture roughly in the centre but closer to the edge nearest to you. Form the mixture into a sausage shape. Fold the bottom edge up and over the mixture, tucking it under the mixture securely. Fold the left and right sides over and then continue rolling away from you. If one piece of round rice paper tears then use two, one on top of the other.

10 When all the rolls are ready, heat the oil until hot in a large frying pan. Shallow fry, turning frequently, until the mixture is cooked, taking care not to burn the rice paper. If you wish to deep-fry, put less filling in the rolls to ensure it is thoroughly cooked before the outside burns. Drain on kitchen paper.

11 Place the rolls in the centre of a lettuce leaf, with some mint and coriander. Roll up and dip into the dipping sauce while still hot.

Vegetarian Crystal Vietnamese Rolls

BÌ CUỐN CHAY VIỆT NAM

SERVES 4

The secret is not to wet the Banh Trang too much in case it tears. It will take a bit of practice but it is well worth the effort as guests will be impressed by your efforts.

- **225g/8oz rice vermicelli**
- **4 dried Chinese mushrooms or 8 button mushrooms**
- **2 pieces black wood ear fungus**
- **1 packet round Banh Trang rice paper**
- **2 pickled onions, thinly sliced**
- **2 pickled gherkins, thinly sliced**
- **225g/8oz sliced bamboo shoots, drained and thinly sliced**
- **1 carrot, grated**
- **4 rings fresh pineapple or small can pineapple slices, drained and thinly sliced**

DIPPING SAUCE

- **100ml/4fl oz Nuoc Mam sauce or Maggi liquid seasoning; if using Maggi add 2 tbsp lemon juice**
- **1 clove garlic, crushed**
- **1 small chilli, chopped (optional)**

TO SERVE

- **1 Webbs or round lettuce**
- **sprigs of coriander**
- **sprigs of mint**
- **½ cucumber, peeled and sliced into matchsticks 1¼in/3cm long**

1 Make the dipping sauce by combining all the ingredients and mixing thoroughly

2 Soak the rice vermicelli in boiled water, slightly cooled, until soft. Drain thoroughly.

3 Soak the dried mushrooms and wood ear fungus in boiled water, slightly cooled, until soft. Drain thoroughly and squeeze out excess water. If using buttom mushrooms, wash and dry them thoroughly. Slice thinly.

4 Place a clean tea towel on the surface you are working on. Dip a single sheet of Banh Trang into warm water and place it on the tea towel. It should be soft and pliable but not too wet. Place some vermicelli, dried mushrooms, wood ear fungus, pickled onion, pickled gherkin, bamboo shoots, carrot and pineapple near the centre but towards the bottom edge.

5 Spread the filling into a sausage shape. Roll the bottom edge of the Banh Trang up and tuck tightly under the mixture. Fold the left and right sides into the centre and continue rolling away from you. Continue until all the mixture is used.

6 Place the vegetarian rolls on a dish. The guests help themselves to lettuce leaves, one at a time. On the lettuce they place a roll, some mint, coriander and cucumber. They then roll everything up and dip it in the dipping sauce.

Prawn and Minced Pork on Sugar Cane

CHAO TÔM VÓI THIT LON XAY

SERVES 4

- **1 tbsp dried prawns or shrimps (optional)**
- **225g/8oz peeled prawns**
- **175g/6oz pork, minced**
- **1 small onion, finely chopped**
- **2 tbsp coriander leaves, finely chopped**
- **salt and pepper**
- **15ml/1 tbsp Nuoc Mam sauce or 15ml/1 tbsp Maggi liquid seasoning mixed with 8ml/½ tbsp lemon juice, 2 crushed anchovies or 8ml/½ tbsp anchovy essence, 1 garlic clove, crushed and dried, and ¼ spring onion, finely chopped**
- **1 egg, beaten**
- **4 × 15cm/6in lengths of sugar cane or bamboo skewers**
- **plain flour or cornflour (optional)**
- **vegetable oil for deep-frying (optional)**
- **Webbs lettuce**

1 If using dried prawns or shrimps, soak for about 1 hour in warm water. Squeeze out excess water and chop finely. Wash the fresh prawns and chop finely.

2 Put the minced pork into a large bowl. Add the onion, coriander, fresh and dried prawns or shrimps, salt and pepper and Nuoc Mam sauce.

3 Pour the egg into the pork and prawn mixture and mix well with your hand. The mixture should come together so that it can be moulded around the lengths of sugar cane or around bamboo skewers. If it is too runny, sift a little plain flour or cornflour into the mixture.

4 Peel the sugar cane, leaving 2.5cm/1in of the green covering on at each end, or 5cm/2in at one end. Mould the mixture on to the peeled part of the sugar cane.

5 Grill the sticks under a moderately hot grill, turning to ensure evenness in the cooking. Make sure that the sugar cane does not burn. Alternatively, deep-fry in hot oil for 4–5 minutes.

6 Serve on a bed of lettuce. The sugar cane should be chewed or sucked as you eat the prawn and pork.

Vegetarian Vietnamese Spring Rolls

BÁNH CUỐN CHAY VIÊT NAM

SERVES 6

Vegetarian friends have enthused over these rolls. It is important to use ingredients that will not break through the delicate rice paper – that is why the ingredients must be minced, cut or grated finely. There must be no sharp edges. Once you have practised with these ingredients you could go on to substitute any of them with other vegetable ingredients.

- **175g/6oz bean thread vermicelli**
- **4 dried Chinese mushrooms or 6 button mushrooms**
- **1 piece light or yellow wood ear fungus**
- **1 piece black wood ear fungus**
- **1 small can water chestnuts, drained and chopped**
- **2 cloves garlic, minced**
- **2 carrots, grated**
- **2 onions, grated**
- **15ml/1 tbsp Nuoc Mam sauce or 15ml/1 tbsp light soya sauce mixed with 2 anchovies or 8ml/½ tbsp anchovy essence and a dash of lime or lemon juice**
- **black pepper**
- **1 egg, beaten**
- **1 packet of quadrant-shaped or round Banh Trang rice paper**
- **vegetable oil for frying**

DIPPING SAUCE

- **125ml/¼ pt Nuoc Mam sauce or 60ml/4 tbsp Maggi liquid seasoning**
- **1 clove garlic, finely chopped**
- **1 red chilli pepper, finely chopped**
- **10ml/2 tsp lemon or lime juice**
- **5ml/1 tsp cider vinegar or wine vinegar**
- **1 tsp sugar**
- **50g/2oz grated peanuts (optional)**

TO SERVE

- **1 Webbs or round lettuce**
- **sprigs of coriander**
- **sprigs of mint**
- **½ cucumber, peeled and cut into matchstick slices**

1 Make the dipping sauce first. Combine all the ingredients and stir thoroughly.

2 Soak the vermicelli in boiled water, slightly cooled, until soft. Drain thoroughly. Use kitchen scissors to cut into shorter strands.

3 Soak the Chinese mushrooms and the light and black wood ear fungus in boiled water, slightly cooled. When soft drain thoroughly, gently squeezing out any excess water. Cut finely. If using button mushrooms, wash, drain and chop finely.

4 Place the vermicelli, water chestnuts, garlic, carrot, onion, light and black wood ear fungus, Nuoc Mam sauce, black pepper and egg in a large mixing bowl. With your hands, mix and knead the mixture until it is stiff enough to be shaped. Follow the same method to make and fry the rolls as for Vietnamese Spring Rolls (page 32).

5 Place the rolls in the centre of a lettuce leaf with some mint, coriander and cucumber. Roll up and dip into the sauce while still hot.

Chicken Saté

SA-TÊ GÀ

SERVES 4

- ★ **30ml/2 tbsp coconut cream or plain yogurt**
- ★ **1 clove garlic, crushed**
- ★ **1 tsp chilli powder**
- ★ **1 tsp ground cumin**
- ★ **1 tsp ground coriander**
- ★ **15ml/1 tbsp lemon juice**
- ★ **225g/8oz fresh chicken, cubed**

DIPPING SAUCE

- ★ **30ml/2 tbsp coconut cream or plain yogurt**
- ★ **1 clove garlic, crushed**
- ★ **½ tsp ground cumin**
- ★ **1 tsp ground ginger**
- ★ **1 tsp ground coriander**
- ★ **15ml/1 tbsp lemon juice**
- ★ **1 tbsp chopped fresh mint**

1 Combine the coconut cream or yogurt with the garlic, chilli powder, cumin, coriander and lemon juice. Marinate the chicken pieces in the mixture for at least 4 hours, turning frequently.

2 Make the dipping sauce by mixing all the ingredients except the mint thoroughly. Leave to blend in a cool place.

3 When the chicken is ready, thread it on to four skewers. Place on the barbecue or under a preheated high grill and cook until well done, basting frequently with the marinade and turning.

4 Heat the dipping sauce and toss in the mint leaves. Serve separately.

Beef Saté

SA-TÊ BÒ

SERVES 4

- ★ **2 cloves garlic, crushed and sliced**
- ★ **1 tsp fresh basil**
- ★ **1 red chilli pepper, sliced**
- ★ **15ml/1 tbsp lime juice**
- ★ **15ml/1 tbsp sesame oil**
- ★ **15ml/1 tbsp Nuoc Mam sauce (optional)**
- ★ **225g/8oz steak, cubed**

DIPPING SAUCE

- ★ **45ml/3 tbsp Nuoc Mam sauce or 30ml/2 tbsp Maggi liquid seasoning**
- ★ **15ml/1 tbsp lime or lemon juice**
- ★ **1 pickled onion, thinly sliced**
- ★ **1 clove garlic, finely chopped**
- ★ **1 tbsp peanuts, finely chopped**

1 Mix the garlic, basil, chilli, lime juice, sesame oil and Nuoc Mam sauce, if using, together. Marinate the cubes of beef in this for at least 4 hours, turning frequently.

2 Make the dipping sauce by mixing all the ingredients thoroughly and place in a bowl on the table.

3 When the beef is ready, thread on to four skewers and place on the barbecue or under a preheated high grill until cooked, turning frequently. Baste equally frequently with the marinade.

Women usually squat like this to sell their products or pass the time of day.

Prawn and Scallop Saté

SA-TÊ TÔM VÀ SÒ

SERVES 4

Saté was probably introduced into Vietnam by traders from India. Bite-sized pieces of succulent meat, seafood, poultry or vegetables are seasoned and grilled over charcoal. A dipping sauce is always presented with the saté.

- **150ml/¼ pt dry sherry or dry white wine**
- **15ml/1 tbsp wine vinegar**
- **1 tbsp chopped dill**
- **salt to taste**
- **12 large scallops, washed**
- **12 large prawns in their shells**
- **1 cucumber, cut into 1cm/½in slices**

SPICY TOMATO DIPPING SAUCE

- **1 large onion, finely chopped**
- **30ml/2 tbsp vegetable oil**
- **2 cloves garlic, chopped and crushed**
- **2 fresh red chilli peppers, finely chopped**
- **6 tomatoes, skinned**
- **1 tbsp sweet basil, chopped**

1 Place the sherry, vinegar, dill and salt in a pan and bring to the boil. Reduce the heat to a simmer and add the scallops. Allow to simmer for 2 minutes. Remove the scallops and keep the liquid to use as the baste when barbecuing.

2 Skewer the prawns, cucumber and scallops alternately so that each skewer has three prawns, three scallops and three pieces of cucumber. Leave, covered, in a refrigerator.

3 Gently fry the onions in the oil for 3 minutes. Add the garlic and fry for a further minute. Add the chilli and tomatoes and fry for another 5 minutes. Add the basil leaves and stir. Remove from the heat and leave to cool.

4 Place the saté on the barbecue or under a preheated high grill and cook for 3–4 minutes on each side. Baste frequently with the reserved cooking liquid.

Mushroom Saté

SA-TÉ NÃM

SERVES 4

- 1 clove garlic, crushed
- 1 tsp fresh ginger, minced
- 1 tsp fresh lemon grass, minced or grated lemon rind
- 1 tbsp fresh coriander, chopped
- 30ml/2 tbsp Nuoc Mam sauce (optional)
- 15ml/1 tbsp sesame oil
- 16 firm white button mushrooms

DIPPING SAUCE

- 3 tbsp roasted peanuts or 3 tbsp crunchy peanut butter
- 1 red chilli pepper, finely chopped
- 1 clove garlic, minced
- 1 tbsp mint, finely chopped
- 15ml/1 tbsp lime or lemon juice
- 45ml/3 tbsp Nuoc Mam sauce or 45ml/3 tbsp light soya sauce mixed with 5ml/1 tsp anchovy essence
- 30ml/2 tbsp sesame oil
- 100ml/4fl oz thin coconut milk

1 Mix the garlic, ginger, lemon grass, coriander, Nuoc Mam sauce, if used, and sesame oil. Marinate the mushrooms in the mixture for 3–4 hours, turning frequently.

2 Make the dipping sauce by mixing and pounding all the dipping sauce ingredients together except for the coconut milk. A rough paste should result. Stir in the coconut milk.

3 Thread the mushrooms onto four skewers. Place on the barbecue or under a preheated high grill for about 3 minutes on either side, basting with the marinade. Serve hot with the dipping sauce.

Vietnamese Salad

RAU TRÔN KIÊU VIÊT NAM

SERVES 6

Most meals in Vietnam are accompanied by a salad or salad ingredients. Salads are also eaten as first courses or a side dish. A Vietnamese salad is never plain – Vietnamese are adventurous in their mixing of textures and tastes. We used to have this particular salad on Mondays but it is called the Sunday salad as we used leftover bits of the Sunday joint.

- 2 stalks fresh lemon grass (discard outer leaves), thinly sliced
- 50g/2oz each leftover roast beef, pork, lamb or chicken, finely shredded
- 1 bunch spring onions, washed and finely chopped
- 2 carrots, finely grated
- 1 red chilli pepper, finely sliced
- 2 cloves garlic, finely sliced and crushed
- 45ml/3 tbsp Nuoc Mam sauce or 30ml/2 tbsp Maggi liquid seasoning mixed with 5ml/1 tsp anchovy essence
- 135ml/9 tbsp lime or lemon juice
- 2 tbsp fresh basil, chopped
- 2 tbsp coriander, finely chopped

1 Lightly hit the sliced lemon grass with the back of a cleaver or heavy knife to release the flavour and smell. Mix the lemon grass with the leftover meat then add the spring onions and toss well. Mix in the grated carrot.

2 Mix together the chilli, garlic, Nuoc Mam sauce and lime juice and stir well. Add to the salad and toss well. Throw in the basil and coriander and toss again. If you think you need more salad dressing, add equal parts of Nuoc Mam sauce and lime juice.

Minced Meat, Crab and Grapefruit Vietnamese Salad

RAU TRÔN THIT XAY, CUA VÀ BUOI VIÊT NAM

SERVES 4

- ★ **175g/6oz minced pork or minced beef**
- ★ **45ml/3 tbsp water**
- ★ **30ml/2 tbsp lime or lemon juice**
- ★ **30ml/2 tbsp Nuoc Mam sauce or 30ml/2 tbsp Maggi liquid seasoning mixed with 5ml/1 tsp anchovy essence**
- ★ **1 green chilli pepper, finely sliced**
- ★ **1 small Spanish onion, finely diced**
- ★ **1cm/½in fresh root ginger, finely chopped**
- ★ **1 tbsp fresh coriander, finely chopped**
- ★ **1 small can crab meat, thoroughly drained**
- ★ **1 Pomelo or pink grapefruit, segmented then halved**

GARNISH

- ★ **lettuce leaves**
- ★ **grated carrot**

1 Place the minced meat in the water and slowly cook over a medium heat until the meat turns colour and is just cooked but still tender. Remove from the heat and leave to cool slightly.

2 Add the lime juice, Nuoc Mam sauce and chilli to the meat. When thoroughly cooled, add the onion, ginger, coriander and crab meat and stir thoroughly. Toss the grapefruit into the salad.

3 Place the lettuce leaves on a flat dish. Arrange the grated carrot on the lettuce to form a ring. Spoon the salad into the centre of the carrot.

Simple Salad

RAU TRÔN DON GIAN

SERVES 4

- **1 lettuce, finely shredded**
- **1 cucumber, peeled and cut lengthways into thin strips**
- **2 carrots, peeled and cut lengthways into thin strips**
- **1 large handful of beansprouts, washed and drained thoroughly**
- **3 tbsp fresh coriander, chopped**
- **3 tbsp fresh mint, chopped**
- **2 hard-boiled eggs, quartered, to garnish**

SALAD DRESSING

- **60ml/4 tbsp Nuoc Mam sauce or 45ml/3 tbsp Maggi liquid seasoning**
- **60ml/4 tbsp lemon juice**
- **15ml/1 tbsp wine vinegar**
- **3 cloves garlic, finely chopped and crushed**
- **1 tsp sugar**
- **1 red chilli pepper, finely chopped**
- **3 tbsp crushed roasted peanuts**

1 Combine the lettuce, cucumber, carrots and beansprouts. Mix lightly.

2 Mix the Nuoc Mam sauce, lemon juice and vinegar. Add the garlic and sugar and stir thoroughly, then add the chilli and peanuts and stir again.

3 Toss the dressing into the salad and scatter the coriander and mint over the top. Garnish with the egg quarters.

The main way to travel quickly and efficiently through the many inland waterways, especially in South Vietnam, is by water "taxi".

Vietnamese Pancake

BANH XEO

SERVES 2

The Banh Xeo or Vietnamese fried pancake or omelette reflects the Indian influence in Vietnamese cuisine. Traditionally, the thin batter made with a rice flour would be poured through a thin piece of muslin. The batter would be steamed quickly and then scraped off and folded around a filling. It is neither practical nor easy to do and so I use the basic filling and an ordinary omelette pan. This omelette can be eaten on its own as part of a mixed array of starters or left to cool, cut into strips and placed as a garnish on noodles, salad or rice dishes.

- **3 eggs**
- **10ml/1–2 tsp Nuoc Mam sauce (optional)**
- **15ml/1 tbsp vegetable oil**
- **1–2 tsp dried prawns, soaked in warm water until soft and drained or 10 shelled prawns**
- **1 tsp fresh mint, finely chopped**
- **1 tsp fresh coriander, finely chopped**

1 Beat the eggs with the Nuoc Mam sauce until light and fluffy.

2 In an omelette pan, heat the oil over a medium heat. Add the egg and Nuoc Mam sauce mixture. Before it sets, stir in the prawns, mint and coriander. Continue cooking until set.

3 To finish off the top and obtain a successful rise, finish off under a preheated high grill. Ease around with a wooden spatula and fold the omelette.

Simple Salad ▶

Banh Xeo Stuffed with Minced Pork and Beansprouts

BÁNH XÉO VỚI NHÂN THIT LON XAY VÀ GIA

SERVES 4

- **30ml/2 tbsp vegetable oil**
- **1 clove garlic, finely chopped**
- **1 small onion, finely chopped**
- **175g/6oz minced pork**
- **1 handful beansprouts, washed and drained**
- **3 eggs**
- **5–10ml/1–2 tsp Nuoc Mam sauce (optional)**

1 Heat half the vegetable oil in an omelette pan or a wok. Quickly fry the garlic and onion until the aromas are released. Add the pork and stir-fry until brown.

2 Toss in the beansprouts and stir-fry for 2–3 minutes. The beansprouts should maintain their crunchiness. Remove from the heat, cover and keep warm.

3 Beat the eggs with the Nuoc Mam sauce until light and fluffy. In an omelette pan, heat the remaining oil over a medium heat and pour in the egg and Nuoc Mam sauce. When the omelette begins to set, put the pork and beansprout mixture into the centre and fold the sides over to form a square.

4 To finish off the top and obtain a successful rise, finish off under a preheated high grill.

Crab and Corn Porridge

CHÁO BAP VÓI THIT CUA

SERVES 4

Corn is grown throughout Vietnam and crabs are caught daily and sold cheaply in the market. If you want, fresh corn and crab can be used, but the recipe I give here saves time by using canned products. The result is just as good.

- **600ml/1 pt basic chicken stock or 1 can condensed cream of chicken soup**
- **300g/11oz can sweet corn kernels**
- **300g/11oz can creamed sweet corn**
- **300g/11oz can crab meat, drained**
- **1 egg**
- **2 spring onions, cut into thin rings**

1 If using condensed soup, add 2 cans of water and milk mixed. Bring the stock or soup to just below boiling point.

2 Roughly chop the sweet corn kernels or leave whole. Add the sweet corn kernels and the creamed sweet corn to the stock. Add the crab meat and stir thoroughly.

3 Beat the egg quickly and, holding a fork over the broth, pour the beaten egg along the back of the fork head, moving the fork in a circular motion at the same time. Remove from the heat and cover. Allow to set for about 40 seconds.

4 Sprinkle with the spring onions, stir once and serve hot.

Deep Fried Fish Cakes

CHA CÁ CHIÊN

SERVES 4

In Vietnam a milkfish or pomfret might be used for this recipe. I have found frozen cod fillets or coley fillets perfectly adequate substitutes here.

- ★ **275g/10oz white fish**
- ★ **150ml/¼ pt coconut milk or cow's milk**
- ★ **225g/8oz sweet potatoes, boiled and mashed**
- ★ **2 tomatoes, skinned and chopped**
- ★ **2 tbsp coriander, chopped**
- ★ **30ml/2 tbsp Nuoc Mam sauce or 30ml/2 tbsp light soya sauce mixed with 5ml/1 tsp anchovy essence**
- ★ **2 eggs, lightly beaten**
- ★ **rice flour or plain flour**
- ★ **vegetable oil for deep-frying**

GARNISH

- ★ **lettuce leaves**
- ★ **sprigs of mint**

1 Cover the fish with the coconut milk. (If there is not sufficient add a little water or cow's milk.) Bring the milk to the boil and simmer for 10 minutes or until the fish is tender. Remove any skin or bones and flake the fish.

2 Place the fish, potato, tomatoes and coriander in a bowl and mix well.

3 Combine the Nuoc Mam sauce and egg. Add half this mixture slowly to the fish mixture so that it retains its shape. Add some flour if the mixture is too runny.

4 Shape the mixture into small balls. Dip each ball into the remaining egg and Nuoc Mam sauce mixture and roll into the rice flour.

5 Heat the oil until it is smoking and deep-fry until the balls are golden brown.

6 Serve hot, garnished with the lettuce and sprigs of mint.

Roasted Spare Ribs with Lemon Grass and Chilli

THIT SUÒN NUÓNG VOI SA VÀ ÓT

SERVES 4

- 12 pork spare ribs
- 30ml/2 tbsp clear honey
- 1 tsp five-spice powder
- 2 cloves garlic, finely chopped and crushed
- 45ml/3 tbsp dry sherry or rice wine
- 45ml/3 tbsp Nuoc Mam sauce or 45ml/3 tbsp light soya sauce mixed with 5ml/1 tsp anchovy essence
- 2 stalks fresh lemon grass, sliced thinly, or grated rind of 1 lemon
- 2 fresh red chilli peppers, finely chopped

1 Wash and dry the spare ribs and place them in a large bowl.

2 In another bowl, combine the honey, five-spice powder, garlic, dry sherry, Nuoc Mam, lemon grass and chilli. Mix well. Spread the honey mixture over the spare ribs and leave to marinate for 4 hours.

3 The ribs can be cooked over a barbecue, turning frequently and basting with the marinade; or baked in the oven at 190°C/375°F/Gas Mark 5, basting with the marinade; or grilled under a moderately hot grill, basting with the marinade.

FISH DISHES

Fried Eel with Lemon Grass and Peanut

LUON XÀO VÓI SA VÁ LAC

SERVES 4

Freshwater and saltwater eels are popular throughout Vietnam and, indeed, Asia in general. The fishmonger will clean and fillet the eel for you. The hot sesame seed oil will spread out below the eel, adding a subtle nutty flavour that is echoed by the topping of the crunchy crushed nuts.

- ★ **vegetable oil for deep-frying**
- ★ **450g/1lb cleaned and filleted eel, cut into strips 5cm/2in long and 15mm/⅜in thick**
- ★ **2 stalks lemon grass, cleaned and cut into strips**
- ★ **150ml/¼ pt chicken stock**
- ★ **30ml/2 tbsp Nuoc Mam sauce or 30ml/2 tbsp Maggi liquid seasoning mixed with 5ml/1 tsp anchovy essence**
- ★ **15ml/1 tbsp rice wine or dry sherry**
- ★ **1 tsp sugar**
- ★ **1 tsp cornflour mixed with a little cold water**
- ★ **15ml/1 tbsp sesame seed oil**
- ★ **2 tbsp crushed roasted peanuts, to garnish**

1 Heat the oil until hot and deep-fry the pieces of eel until crisp and golden brown. Drain on kitchen paper and set aside.

2 Mix the lemon grass, chicken stock, Nuoc Mam sauce, rice wine and sugar and heat in a saucepan. Just at boiling point, add the fried eel pieces, cover, and simmer for 3 minutes. Stir in the cornflour mixture to thicken.

3 Place on a dish in a ring shape, leaving a well in the centre. Heat the sesame oil until very hot and pour this into the well. Sprinkle the crushed roasted peanuts as a garnish.

Grilled Bass with Ginger Sauce

CÁ BASS NUÓNG VÓI XÔT GÙNG

SERVES 4

Bass, perch or carp can be used for this recipe. Fishing is a major industry in Vietnam, where the farmed fish are mainly species of the tailapia, carp, catfish and snakehead.

- ★ **1 bass, large enough to serve 4, cleaned and gutted**
- ★ **juice from 2 limes**
- ★ **2 tbsp dill, chopped**
- ★ **15ml/1 tbsp sesame oil**
- ★ **1 piece Chinese stem ginger, cut into strips, to garnish**

GINGER SAUCE

- ★ **2 dried Chinese mushrooms, soaked until soft, drained and thinly sliced with stalks removed, or 4 button mushrooms, thinly sliced**
- ★ **2 stalks lemon grass, peeled and thinly sliced**
- ★ **2 spring onions, finely chopped**
- ★ **1 red chilli pepper, thinly sliced**
- ★ **90ml/3½oz supermarket brand ginger wine**
- ★ **15ml/1 tbsp Nuoc Mam sauce or 15ml/1 tbsp light soya sauce**
- ★ **1 piece Chinese stem ginger, cut into strips (optional)**
- ★ **30ml/2 tbsp wine vinegar**
- ★ **60ml/4 tbsp water**
- ★ **1 tbsp cornflour mixed with a little water**

1 Rub the bass with the remnants of the limes. Make slanting slashes down both sides of the fish. Pour the lime juice over the fish. Sprinkle over the dill and leave covered in the refrigerator for 2–4 hours.

2 Simmer all the ginger sauce ingredients except the cornflour together for at least 3 minutes. Gently add in the cornflour, stirring all the time. You should see the mixture thicken. Turn off the heat and cover.

3 Brush both sides of the bass with sesame oil. On a barbecue or under a preheated hot grill, cook the fish until just done.

4 Serve the fish hot with the ginger sauce poured over it. Garnish with stem ginger.

Small fishing boats at rest at the end of the day.

Carp Cooked in Coconut Milk

Cá Chép Nâu Vói Nuóc Dùa

SERVES 4

This recipe works well with any firm fish steak. Try it with cod, halibut or trout.

- ★ 15ml/1 tbsp vegetable oil
- ★ 1 stalk lemon grass, peeled and finely chopped
- ★ ½ tsp peppercorns, bruised
- ★ 1 clove garlic, chopped and crushed
- ★ 1 red chilli pepper, thinly sliced
- ★ ½ tbsp ground cinnamon
- ★ 4 whole cloves, bruised
- ★ 30ml/2 tbsp Nuoc Mam sauce or 30ml/2 tbsp light soya sauce
- ★ 120ml/4½fl oz coconut milk
- ★ 1 carp, large enough to serve 4, cleaned and gutted
- ★ rind and juice of 1 lime
- ★ 1 tbsp fresh coriander, finely chopped

1 In the oil, gently fry the lemon grass, peppercorns, garlic, chilli, cinnamon and cloves until the flavour is released – 2 minutes at the outside.

2 Add the Nuoc Mam sauce and stir in gently. Remove from the heat and stir in the coconut milk.

3 Place the carp in a pan and pour over the coconut milk mixture. Add the lime juice and fresh coriander and stir. Cover and simmer for 10–15 minutes or until the fish is cooked.

4 Remove the fish and place on a serving dish. Garnish with the strips of lime rind. Heat the sauce and boil for a few minutes to reduce and thicken. Strain until a plain milk is left. Pour this over the carp.

Steamed Crab with Light Wine Sauce

Cua Hâp Vói Nuóc Xôt Có Ruou

SERVES 4

Vietnamese people eat crabs a lot as they are plentiful and inexpensive; they are found in the lakes, rivers, mangrove swamps and coastal waters. The freshwater crab is highly prized for its delicious, sweet-flavoured meat. The choicest meat comes from the tender claw, the most delicate part is the rich orange roe. Vietnamese cooks in the home prepare crab in a variety of ways.

- ★ 700g/1½lb crab claws
- ★ 2 stalks lemon grass, peeled and finely chopped, or grated rind of 1 lemon
- ★ 1 slice fresh root ringer, peeled and finely chopped

SAUCE

- ★ 60ml/4 tbsp rice wine, dry sherry or dry white wine
- ★ 15ml/1 tbsp Nuoc Mam sauce or 15ml/1 tbsp light soya sauce
- ★ 15ml/1 tbsp sesame seed oil
- ★ 1 tbsp lemon grass, finely chopped
- ★ ½ tbsp spring onions, finely chopped

1 Break open the crab claws by placing a newspaper on top and tapping with the back of a cleaver or a steak mallet. Carefully extract the flesh and discard any shell and cartilage. Place in a bowl and flake with a fork.

2 Add the lemon grass and ginger. Mix well, cover and steam for about 15 minutes.

3 Mix together the sauce ingredients and serve separately.

A freshly caught batch of fish – delicious fried or barbecued.

Scallops Stuffed with Shrimp Paste

SÒ DÔN CHA TÔM

SERVES 4

- **12 scallops, cleaned**
- **vegetable oil for frying**

SHRIMP PASTE STUFFING

- **1 tbsp dried shrimps, soaked in water until soft, drained and finely chopped or 20 defrosted frozen prawns, finely chopped**
- **2 small pieces of black wood ear fungus, soaked in warm water until soft, drained and finely chopped**
- **100g/4oz sweet potato, boiled and mashed**
- **15ml/1 tbsp Nuoc Mam sauce or 15ml/1 tbsp light soya sauce**

1 Make the shrimp paste stuffing by combining all the stuffing ingredients together.

2 Steam the scallops until cooked – about 5 minutes in a bamboo steamer. Remove and leave to cool.

3 Slit the scallops in their thickest part and spoon in the stuffing. Heat the oil until very hot. Gently lower the stuffed scallops in a basket and fry for 2 minutes.

Scallops Grilled in Pork Fat with Nuoc Mam Sauce

Sò Nuóng Vói Mo Heo Ăn Vói Nuóc Măm

SERVES 4

- **4 scallops, cleaned**
- **½ tsp salt**
- **juice of 1 lime or lemon**
- **1 piece pork belly fat or rind of 8 bacon rashers**
- **60ml/4 tbsp Nuoc Mam sauce or 60ml/4 tbsp Maggi liquid seasoning mixed with 30ml/2 tbsp lemon juice, 1 clove garlic, diced, and ½ spring onion, thinly chopped**

1 Cover the scallops with water and add the salt and lime or lemon juice. Simmer for 1–2 minutes (do not overcook). Remove the scallops from the liquid and drain them.

2 Place each scallop in a shell or heatproof dish, place some belly pork or bacon rind on the scallops and put under a preheated high grill for at most 4 minutes. The pork fat should drip down on to the scallops, giving them a smoky pork flavour. Remove and serve with the Nuoc Mam sauce.

Deep Fried Squid with Plantain/Banana Fritters

MUC CHIÊN VÓI CHUÔI CHIÊN

SERVES 4

- **450g/1lb fresh squid, cleaned and prepared**
- **2 large cloves garlic, minced**
- **10ml/2 tsp Nuoc Mam sauce (optional)**
- **2 tbsp chopped fresh dill**
- **black pepper**
- **cornflour**
- **vegetable oil for deep-frying**

NUOC CHAM SAUCE

- **2 small cloves garlic, crushed**
- **1 small fresh red chilli pepper, seeded and minced**
- **25g/1oz sugar**
- **30ml/2 tbsp fresh lime or lemon juice**
- **50ml/2fl oz cider vinegar or wine vinegar**
- **50ml/2fl oz Nuoc Mam sauce or Maggi liquid seasoning**
- **15ml/1 tbsp water**

PLANTAIN FRITTERS

- **1 egg**
- **25g/1oz caster sugar**
- **1 whole ripe plantain, peeled and mashed**
- **50g/2oz plain flour**
- **1 tsp baking powder**
- **vegetable oil for frying**

BATTER

- **100g/4oz plain flour**
- **pinch of salt**
- **pinch of ground cinnamon**
- **1 egg, beaten**
- **150ml/¼ pt milk**

1 Make the fritters first. Make the batter by mixing the flour and salt. Stir the cinnamon, egg and milk together and add to the flour and salt mixture. Mix thoroughly using a wire whisk. Place on a low shelf in the refrigerator for at least 30 minutes.

2 Add the egg and then 25g/1oz sugar to the plantain, beating continuously. Mix the flour and baking powder, stir into the plantain mixture and blend thoroughly. Coat the mixture, a tablespoon at a time, with the batter. Heat the oil and fry these one at a time. Set the fritters aside.

3 Make the Nuoc Cham sauce. Place the garlic, chilli, sugar, lime or lemon juice, vinegar, Nuoc Mam sauce and water in a blender or food processor and blend for 30 seconds or until the sugar dissolves. Set aside.

4 Separate the head and body of the squid by pulling apart gently. Cut off and chop up the tentacles; discard the head. Peel off the membrane from the body. Wash the squid under cold water and cut the body into rings.

5 Combine the squid, tentacles, garlic, Nuoc Mam sauce, if used, dill and black pepper. Allow to marinate for 30 minutes. Coat the rings and tentacles in cornflour, shaking off excess.

6 Heat the oil until it starts to smoke. Drop in the squid pieces a few at a time and deep-fry for about 1 minute or until golden brown. Remove and drain on absorbent kitchen paper.

7 On a serving plate, make a ring with the plantain fritters and heap the deep-fried squid in the middle. Serve hot with the Nuoc Cham sauce in a small bowl.

Crab Stuffed with Minced Pork and Coriander

CUA TRÔN VÓI THIT LON XAY VÀ NGÒ

SERVES 4

- **2 cooked crabs**
- **225g/8oz lean pork, chopped**
- **1 onion, chopped**
- **1 tsp black pepper**
- **15g/½oz sugar**
- **15ml/1 tbsp Nuoc Mam sauce (optional)**
- **1 tbsp coriander root, chopped**
- **2 eggs, separated**
- **1 tbsp spring onions, chopped**
- **1 tbsp fresh coriander leaves, chopped**
- **1 fresh red or green chilli pepper, finely sliced**

1 Remove the limbs from the crabs. Remove the flesh from the shells, taking care to keep them intact. Remove the flesh from the limbs as well. Flake all the flesh and set aside.

2 Combine the pork, onion, pepper, sugar, Nuoc Mam sauce, if used, and coriander root in a food processor or blender. Remove and place in a bowl. Add the crab meat and egg white. Add the spring onions and coriander leaves and mix by hand, using more egg white if necessary.

3 Fill the crab shells with the mixture to form a generous mound. Carefully break the egg yolk and place ½ tsp yolk on the top of each mound. Sprinkle with chilli. Be very careful when moving the crab shells or else the yolk will run. (If you think this is too difficult, brush the filling with the beaten egg yolk and sprinkle with the sliced chilli and some coriander leaves.)

4 Place each crab, stuffed side up, in a large steamer and steam for 20 minutes. Serve with a generous green salad or Simple Salad (page 40).

Stir-fried Seafood with Mint, Garlic and Chillies

THÚC ĂN BIÊN XÀO VÓI RAU THOM, TOI VÀ ÓT

SERVES 4

- **100g/4oz fish fillets**
- **6 mussels**
- **1 small uncooked crab, cleaned and chopped**
- **100g/4oz squid pieces**
- **100g/4oz uncooked prawns**
- **100g/4oz scallops**
- **2 cloves garlic, chopped**
- **2 large fresh chilli peppers, chopped**
- **1 tbsp coriander root, chopped**
- **50ml/1 tbsp vegetable oil**
- **30ml/2 tbsp oyster sauce**
- **30ml/2 tbsp Nuoc Mam sauce or light soya sauce and 5ml/1 tsp anchovy sauce, mixed well**
- **1 sweet pepper, cut in strips**
- **1 onion, thinly sliced**
- **2 shallots, thinly sliced**
- **4 tbsp fresh mint, chopped**

1 Wash and prepare the seafood. Cut the fish fillets into bite-sized pieces. Scrub the mussels and remove the beards. Take the limbs off the crab and crack the shell with a hammer so the meat is easy to remove at the table. Remove the outer shell, clean out the crab body and break into bite-sized pieces. Set aside.

2 Put the garlic, chillies and coriander root in a blender and make a coarse paste. Put to one side.

3 Heat the oil and fry the garlic, chilli and coriander over medium heat. Add the seafood and stir-fry gently so the fish fillet does not break up. Add the oyster sauce and Nuoc Mam sauce. Taste, cover and simmer for a few minutes.

4 Remove the lid and add the sweet pepper, onion, shallots and mint and stir-fry gently (the fish fillets are now even more delicate) for a couple of minutes then remove from the heat.

5 Arrange on a large, shallow serving dish and garnish with whatever herbs you happen to have around. Serve with a large bowl of steaming rice.

Lobster and Sweet Potato Curry

CÁ-RI TÔM HÙM VỚI KHOAI LANG

SERVES 4–6

- 25g/1oz unsalted butter
- 450g/1lb sweet potatoes, peeled and cut into 2.5cm/1in cubes
- 15ml/1 tbsp sake or dry sherry
- 1 whole lobster, chopped into 2.5cm/1in cubes

CURRY SAUCE

- 15ml/1 tbsp vegetable oil
- 50g/2oz chopped onion
- 1 tbsp garlic, minced
- 2 tsp shrimp paste
- 1 dried chilli, seeds removed, crushed
- 2 tsp cumin seeds
- 1 tbsp coriander seeds
- 1 tsp dried lemon grass, sliced
- 1 tsp ground galangal
- 2 tsp lemon rind, minced
- 2 tbsp fresh coriander, chopped
- 1 tsp salt
- 1 tsp ground turmeric
- 2 tsp sweet paprika

1 Make the curry sauce by heating the oil over medium-high heat. Add the onion and garlic and cook for 5 minutes or until soft. Add the shrimp paste and stir thoroughly, pressing the paste to blend it well. Cook for a further 3 or so minutes and remove from the heat.

2 Grind the chilli, cumin seeds, coriander seeds and lemon grass until powdery.

3 Place the onion mixture in a blender or food processor and blend until very smooth. Add the ground spices, galangal, lemon rind, fresh coriander, salt, turmeric and paprika. Blend until the mixture becomes a smooth paste. This makes about 50ml/2fl oz curry sauce.

4 Melt the butter over medium heat and add the sweet potatoes. Cook for 15 minutes, taking care the potato does not burn.

5 Stir in the curry sauce and sake together until the curry mixture is dissolved. Add the lobster cubes and cook for 2–3 more minutes.

Mackerel Cooked in a Pot Lined with Belly Pork

CA MA-CA-REN KHO COI THIT BA CHI

SERVES 4

- **2 large mackerel, cleaned**
- **2 pieces bean curd**
- **salt**
- **salt and pepper for seasoning**
- **45ml/3 tbsp vegetable oil**
- **100g/4oz pork belly, cut into threads**
- **100g/4oz black Chinese mushrooms, soaked in warm water, cut into threads**
- **100g/4oz bamboo shoots, sliced**
- **1 red chilli pepper, chopped**
- **2 slices root ginger, chopped**
- **15ml/1 tbsp dark soya sauce**
- **15ml/1 tbsp Nuoc Mam sauce**
- **8ml/½ tbsp wine**
- **600ml/1 pt water**
- **2 spring onions, chopped**

1 Chop the mackerel into slices about 2.5cm/1in thick.

2 Wash the bean curds gently with water, salt lightly to absorb the water and season. Cut the bean curds in half and then cut them into cubes.

3 Heat a wok and pour in 15ml/1 tbsp oil to fry the bean curd cubes. Set aside. Heat 15ml/1 tbsp oil and fry the mackerel until both sides turn golden brown.

4 Add the remaining oil. Add the pork, black mushrooms, bamboo shoots, chilli, root ginger, soya sauce, Nuoc Mam sauce, wine and sugar and stir-fry.

5 Pour the contents of the wok into an earthenware pot or heavy pan, add the water and bring to the boil over a high heat. Reduce the heat to low and braise for 20 minutes. Taste and add the spring onions. Serve in the pot when cooked.

Jellyfish, Chicken and Cucumber Salad

DUA LEO TRÔN VÓI SUÁ VÀ THIT GA

SERVES 4

The recipe for this traditional and well-loved dish was given to me by the chef of Bonjour Vietnam, Fulham Road, London.

- **100g/4oz dried jellyfish**
- **2 cooked chicken breasts, cut into strips**
- **½ cucumber, cut into thin strips**
- **1 tbsp fresh mint, chopped**
- **1 tbsp fresh coriander, chopped**
- **roasted peanuts, crushed, to garnish**

NUOC CHAM SAUCE

- **2 dried hot red chilli, cut into pieces**
- **1 clove garlic, chopped**
- **2 tsp sugar**
- **½ fresh lime**
- **30ml/2 tbsp Nuoc Mam sauce or 30ml/2 tbsp light soya sauce and 5ml/1 tsp anchovy essence**
- **45ml/3 tbsp water**

1 Make the Nuoc Cham sauce by mixing the chillies, garlic and sugar and pounding. Squeeze the lime over the mixture. Add the Nuoc Mam sauce and water and stir thoroughly. Set aside.

2 Soak the jellyfish in hot water for about 30 minutes. Remove and soak in cold water for 2 hours, squeezing constantly to remove the salt.

3 Mix together the jellyfish, chicken and cucumber. Add the mint and coriander. Add the dressing and toss. Sprinkle with the crushed peanuts.

Chicken, Duck Frog and Quail Dishes

Caramelized Chicken Wings with an Orange Sauce

CÁNH GÀ NÂU CA-RA-MEN VÓI XÔT CAM

SERVES 4

This dish should have a slightly nutty, burnt flavour, but be careful not to burn the sugar.

- **8 chicken wings**
- **salt and pepper**
- **30ml/2 tbsp sesame oil**
- **60ml/4 tbsp clear honey**
- **60ml/4 tbsp vegetable oil**
- **25g/1oz caster sugar**
- **shredded rind and juice of 1 orange**

1 Season the chicken wings with salt and pepper. Mix the sesame oil and honey and spread this over the wings.

2 Heat the oil in a heavy-based pan and cook the chicken wings for about 4 minutes on each side or until just done. Remove the pan and keep warm. Reserve the pan juices.

3 Add the sugar to the pan and heat without stirring until it caramelizes. Remove from the heat.

4 Add the orange juice and reserved pan juices. Stir over a low heat until a smooth sauce forms, adding a little water or orange juice if it becomes too thick. Add half the orange rind and continue to cook over a very low heat.

5 Place the chicken wings on to a warmed dish. Pour the caramel sauce over them and garnish with the leftover strips of orange.

Stuffed Chicken Wings

CÁNH GÀ DÔN

SERVES 4

This recipe was given to me by the delightful Madame Binh of Thanh Binh, Chalk Farm Road, London. It is a delicious and economical dish, which looks very impressive.

- **8 chicken wings**

STUFFING

- **100g/4oz bean thread vermicelli**
- **3 pieces dark wood ear fungus**
- **275g/10oz pork, minced**
- **1 small onion, grated finely**
- **1 small carrot, grated finely**
- **1 egg, beaten**
- **15ml/1 tbsp Nuoc Mam sauce or light soya sauce**
- **salt and black pepper**

1 Bone the chicken wings by cutting around the bone with a sharp knife. Holding the wingtip, gently ease the bone away to leave the skin and a thin layer of chicken.

2 Soak the vermicelli in warm water for 10 minutes then drain thoroughly and cut into short strands. Soak the wood ear fungus in warm water for 10 minutes then squeeze dry and chop into thin slices.

3 Mix all the stuffing ingredients together. The mixture should be firm. Mould the stuffing into a ball and insert it into the bag of flesh and skin of the chicken wings.

4 Preheat the oven to 200°C/400°F/Gas Mark 6. Steam the stuffed wings for 10–15 minutes. (If you want to make a large quantity, multiply the measures accordingly and freeze after the steaming stage.)

5 After steaming, place in a lightly oiled roasting pan and roast in the oven for 30 minutes. Serve on a bed of lettuce as a starter or with rice and a beef stir-fried dish.

Spicy Barbecued Chicken Legs

CHÂN GÀ NÂU VỚI GIA VỊ

SERVES 4

- 4 chicken legs, preferably from corn-fed chickens
- 15ml/1 tbsp sesame oil

MARINADE

- 30ml/2 tbsp vegetable oil
- 3 cloves garlic, crushed
- 4 spring onions, finely chopped
- 1 stalk lemon grass, finely chopped
- 2 red or green chilli peppers, finely chopped or ½ tsp cayenne pepper
- 15ml/1 tbsp Nuoc Mam sauce or Maggi liquid seasoning
- 1 tsp sugar
- salt

LEMON DIP

- 2 tsp salt
- freshly ground black pepper
- 2 lemons, cut in quarters

1 Place the chicken legs on a wooden board and, using a sharp knife, stab them in several places. This helps them absorb the marinade and prevents the skin from breaking.

2 Make the marinade by heating the vegetable oil and adding the garlic, spring onions and lemon grass. Cook for 2–3 minutes and leave to cool. Stir in the chilli, Nuoc Mam sauce, sugar and salt.

3 Put the chicken legs in a shallow dish and pour the marinade over. Cover the dish and marinate for 2 hours, turning from time to time.

4 Brush liberally with sesame oil and put on a barbecue or under a preheated moderate grill for 15–20 minutes, turning frequently and brushing with oil.

5 Serve immediately with lemon dip and pickled vegetables. Guests make their own dip by mixing salt and pepper and moistening with a quarter of lemon.

Fresh Chicken Salad with Grapefruit, Mint and Lemon Grass

THIT GÀ TRÔN VÓI BUOI, RAU THOM VÀ SA

SERVES 6

- **vegetable oil for deep frying**
- **about 40 prawn chips**
- **1 tbsp unsalted peanuts**
- **1 tbsp sesame seeds**
- **25g/1oz dried prawns, soaked in hot water for 30 minutes**
- **50g/2oz pork belly**
- **50g/2oz uncooked prawns in the shell**
- **salt**
- **1 medium cucumber, unpeeled, halved lengthways, seeded and sliced thinly**
- **1 large carrot, shredded**
- **50g/2oz fresh beansprouts**
- **25g/1oz cooked chicken meat, cut into thin strips**
- **1 tbsp chopped mint**
- **½ tbsp chopped lemon grass**
- **salt**
- **1 large grapefruit, peeled, sectioned and cut crossways into 2.5cm/1in pieces**
- **coriander sprigs, to garnish**

EGG PANCAKES

- **2 eggs**
- **¼ tsp Nuoc Mam sauce**
- **freshly ground black pepper**
- **vegetable oil**

- **1 clove garlic, minced**
- **1 fresh red chilli pepper, seeded and minced**
- **½ tbsp sugar**
- **8ml/½ tbsp fresh lime juice**
- **8ml/½ tbsp rice vinegar**
- **22ml/1½ tbsp Nuoc Mam sauce**

1 Heat about 5cm/2in oil to 180°C/350°F in a wok. Add the chips 2–3 at a time and keep them immersed in the oil with a pair of chopsticks or slotted spoon until puffy. This should take about 10 seconds. Turn and cook for the same length of time. When finished, set aside.

2 Rub down the wok, return it to a moderate heat and cook the peanuts. Stir constantly until the peanuts are golden brown – about 5 minutes. Grind with a grinder or put between a couple of sheets of clean strong paper and grind with a rolling pin or milk bottle. Toast the sesame seeds in the same way for only 3 minutes. Grind lightly to a grainy texture.

3 To make the pancakes, beat the eggs, Nuoc Mam sauce and pepper together with ½ tsp water in a bowl. Brush the bottom of a non-stick omelette pan with some oil and place over moderate heat until hot. Pour in half of the egg mixture and tilt the pan immediately to spread the mixture evenly over the bottom – the pancake should be paper-thin. Cook until the egg is set – this should not take more than 30 seconds. Turn and cook on the other side for about 15 seconds. Set aside. Repeat, using up the rest of the mixture and set aside.

4 Combine the garlic, chilli, sugar, lime juice, vinegar and Nuoc Mam sauce in a bowl. Stir to blend thoroughly. Set the dressing aside.

5 Drain the dried prawns and pound or blend in a blender or processor until very fine. Set aside.

6 Cover the pork with water and bring to the boil over a high heat. Lower and boil for about 30 minutes or until the juices run clear when the meat is pierced with a knife. Run cold water over the pork and set aside.

7 Cook the raw prawns in boiling water until just pink – about 2 minutes. Run cold water over them, drain, peel, de-vein and cut lengthways in halves. Shred the prawns and set aside.

8 Sprinkle salt over the cucumber and carrot and leave to stand for 15 minutes. Run cold water over them and squeeze dry with your hands. It is imperative that the vegetables are bone dry to ensure their crunchiness.

9 Dip the beansprouts in salted boiling water for 30 seconds. Run cold water over them and drain.

10 Cut the egg pancakes into strips. Combine the egg pancake strips, dried prawns, shredded prawns, chicken, cucumber, carrot, beansprouts, mint, lemon grass, grapefruit and sesame seeds. Mix well with your hands and pour over the dressing mixture.

11 Transfer to a serving dish or serve separately, and sprinkle the ground peanuts over it. Garnish with coriander. Serve with prawn chips on which guests place bite-sized portions of the salad. Alternatively, serve in hollowed grapefruit shells instead of a serving dish.

Fresh Chicken with Lemon Grass and Cashew Nuts

THIT GÀ XÀO VÓI SA VÀ DÀO LÔN HÔT

SERVES 4

- vegetable oil
- 2 small dried chillies
- 1 clove garlic, chopped
- 450g/1lb lean, corn-fed chicken, sliced
- ½ tsp sugar
- 15ml/1 tbsp oyster sauce
- 15ml/1 tbsp Nuoc Mam sauce or light soya sauce
- 45ml/3 tbsp chicken stock or water
- 50g/2oz roasted, unsalted cashew nuts
- 1 tbsp lemon grass, chopped
- 2 shallots, cut in quarters

1 With a drop or two of oil, stir-fry the chillies until cooked evenly but not burnt. Set aside.

2 Stir-fry the garlic with a few more drops of oil until golden. Add the chicken slices, sugar and oyster and Nuoc Mam sauces and stir-fry until the chicken is golden in colour. Lower the heat and add the stock. Cook for a few more minutes, stirring occasionally.

3 When the chicken is thoroughly cooked, add the cashew nuts, lemon grass, shallots and chillies and stir several times, being careful not to break the chillies. Remove from the heat and serve.

Chicken with Mango

THIT GÀ VÓI XOAI

SERVES 4

- **450g/1lb corn-fed chicken, cubed**
- **1 large carrot**
- **½ red sweet pepper**
- **½ green sweet pepper**
- **100g/4oz bamboo shoots**
- **1 large mango, just ripe and firm, cut into chunks**
- **60ml/4 tbsp vegetable oil**

MARINADE

- **½ tsp bicarbonate of soda**
- **15g/½oz sugar**
- **1 egg white, lightly beaten**
- **1 tbsp cornflour or potato flour**
- **salt**
- **water**

SAUCE

- **1 tsp sugar**
- **15ml/1 tbsp light soya sauce**
- **15ml/1 tbsp oyster sauce**
- **15ml/1 tbsp sesame seed oil**
- **15ml/1 tbsp rice wine**
- **½ tbsp cornflour or potato flour, mixed with a little water**

1 Mix the marinade ingredients thoroughly and mix well with the chicken pieces. Leave to marinate for 30 minutes.

2 Trim and peel the carrot; cut into matchstick strips a little less than 2.5cm/1in long. Cut the peppers and bamboo shoots into strips to match the carrots. Cut the mango flesh into small, fairly thin pieces as neatly as possible.

3 Heat the oil in a wok and fry the chicken pieces for about 2 minutes. Remove from the oil and drain well. Add the carrot, peppers, mango and bamboo shoots to the hot oil and fry in batches. Remove and drain thoroughly.

4 Rinse and dry the wok, add the chicken and vegetables and stir in all the sauce ingredients except the cornflour. Stir-fry briefly and add the cornflour to the sauce to thicken.

Sun-drenched, palm-lined beaches form the coast of Vietnam.

Chicken Porridge

CHÁO GÀ

SERVES 4 OR MORE

- 50g/2oz long- or short-grained rice
- 1.2 litres/2 pt water
- 225g/8oz corn-fed chicken breast, boned and slivered
- 1 large spring onion, finely chopped
- salt and black pepper
- chopped fresh coriander to garnish

MARINADE

- 30ml/2 tbsp Nuoc Mam sauce, or 30ml/2 tbsp Maggi liquid seasoning
- 1 tsp cornflour dissolved in 30ml/2 tbsp water
- 10ml/2 tsp dry sherry
- salt

1 Rinse and drain the rice. Add the water and bring to the boil over high heat. Turn the heat to medium low, partially cover the pan and let rice bubble for 5 minutes. This loosens the starch and blends the water and rice. Give the rice a stir and turn the heat as low as possible, cover and simmer for about 1 hour.

2 Place the chicken in the marinade for 30 minutes. Add the chicken to the porridge and stir gently. Continue until all the pink in the chicken has disappeared. Turn off the heat, cover and serve in a couple of minutes. Garnish with coriander for more flavour, and spring onion and salt and pepper to taste.

Boiled Chicken with Nuoc Mam Sauce

THIT GÀ LUÔC VÓI NUÓC MĂM

SERVES AT LEAST 6

- **1 large chicken, either corn-fed or free-range**
- **about 2.5 litres/4 pt water**
- **2 × 2.5cm/1in slices peeled root ginger, about 5mm/⅛in thick**
- **30ml/2 tbsp Nuoc Mam sauce or light soya sauce and 1 tsp anchovy essence**
- **12 dried black Chinese mushrooms**
- **15ml/1 tbsp dry sherry**
- **salt**

INDIVIDUAL DIPS

- **15ml/1 tbsp light soya sauce**
- **15ml/1 tbsp sesame seed oil**
- **15ml/1 tbsp Nuoc Mam sauce or 15ml/1 tbsp Maggi liquid seasoning and 3ml/½ tsp anchovy essence**

1 Tear off the fat from the chicken cavity and discard. Cut off the parson's nose and rinse the chicken in cold water. Bring a large pot of water to the boil over high heat and plunge in the chicken. When the water comes to the boil again, let the chicken cook for 1 minute to firm the skin. Remove it and rinse it briefly with running warm water to get rid of any scum.

2 Bring the measured amount of water to the boil with the ginger slices and Nuoc Mam sauce in a deep pot into which the chicken will fit snugly. Add the chicken and, when the water boils again, turn the heat down to a simmer. Cover and simmer for 1½ hours, turning the chicken from time to time to ensure that it cooks evenly.

3 In the meantime, soak the black mushrooms in some warm water for about 20 minutes. Squeeze them dry and rinse in cold water, repeating this a couple of times. Cut off and discard the stems and add the mushrooms to the soup about 30 minutes into the cooking time. Add the sherry when the chicken is cooked and season with salt to taste.

4 Serve the chicken whole in the soup and the dips in individual saucers. Guests tear off pieces of the meat with a fork or chopsticks and put it in their bowls with a little broth and mushrooms. Leftover chicken can be used for a variety of dishes.

Poulet Citron

GÀ NÂU CHANH

SERVES 4

- ★ **2 limes or 3 lemons**
- ★ **½ tsp crushed garlic**
- ★ **1 tbsp root ginger, chopped**
- ★ **2 tbsp lemon grass, chopped**
- ★ **¼ tsp crushed red pepper flakes**
- ★ **15ml/1 tbsp Nuoc Mam sauce**
- ★ **1 large chicken, preferably corn-fed**
- ★ **¼ tsp cayenne pepper**
- ★ **salt**

1 Preheat the oven to 200°C/400°F/Gas Mark 6. Remove the rind from one of the limes with a potato peeler. Mince with the garlic, ginger, lemon grass, red pepper flakes and Nuoc Mam sauce.

2 With your fingers, carefully loosen the skin on the chicken over the breast and legs. Spread the seasoning under the skin as evenly as you can.

3 Mix together the cayenne pepper and salt. Sprinkle some of the mixture in the cavity of the chicken and rub the rest on the skin. Prick both limes – peeled and unpeeled – all over with a fork. Place the limes in the chicken cavity.

4 Place the bird, breast down, in a roasting tin (not on a rack). Roast the chicken for 30 minutes. Then turn the bird breast up and roast for a further hour, basting with the pan juices every 15 minutes.

5 After cooking, let the chicken rest for 5 minutes. Remove, discard the limes, and cut the chicken into bite-sized pieces.

Stewed Chicken Feet with a Mushroom and Spring Onion Sauce

CHAN GÀ HẤP ĂN VỚI XỐT NẤM HÀNH LÁ

SERVES 4

This dish sounds revolting but commands big bucks now in the Vietnamese restaurants of Paris.

- ★ **50g/2oz dried Chinese mushrooms**
- ★ **salt**
- ★ **⅔ tsp sugar**
- ★ **vegetable oil for deep-frying**
- ★ **12 chicken feet, scrubbed, claws trimmed off**
- ★ **30ml/2 tbsp dark soya sauce**
- ★ **3 slices of root ginger, peeled**
- ★ **2 spring onions**
- ★ **2 cloves garlic**
- ★ **parlsey to garnish**

SEASONING

- ★ **15ml/1 tbsp white wine**
- ★ **100ml/4fl oz mushroom water**
- ★ **5ml/1 tsp light soya sauce**
- ★ **5ml/1 tsp oyster sauce**
- ★ **5ml/1 tsp Nuoc Mam sauce (optional)**
- ★ **1 tsp sugar**
- ★ **¼ tsp black pepper**
- ★ **salt**
- ★ **1 tsp cornflour mixed with a little water**

1 Wash the dried Chinese mushrooms and soak them for 2 hours. Squeeze out the excess water and retain as stock. Marinate for ½ hour with salt, sugar and 15ml/1 tbsp oil. Steam for 12 minutes.

2 Blanch the chicken feet in boiling water for 5 minutes. Remove and coat with dark soya sauce. Deep-fry in hot oil until golden. Drain, leaving 30ml/2 tbsp oil for sautéing.

3 Mince the ginger, spring onions and garlic. Heat the reserved oil in a casserole and sauté the ginger, spring onions and garlic until fragrant. Add the chicken feet and stir-fry.

4 In a casserole sizzle the wine, add the mushroom water and seasoning except for the cornflour and stew for an hour. Mix in the mushrooms and simmer for 15 minutes. Remove the lid and thicken the sauce with the cornflour. Serve hot in the casserole, garnished with parsley. Guests suck the meat from the feet.

Garlic Roasted Duck

VIT NÚONG TOI

SERVES 4

- **15ml/1 tbsp Nuoc Mam sauce or light soya sauce**
- **100ml/¼ pt red wine vinegar**
- **1 onion, chopped**
- **12 juniper berries, crushed**
- **2 tsp fennel seeds**
- **1 clove garlic, crushed**
- **4 duck breast and wing portions**
- **150g/5oz tub plain yogurt**
- **salt and black pepper**
- **watercress, to garnish**

1 Mix the Nuoc Mam sauce, vinegar, onion, juniper berries, fennel seeds and garlic thoroughly in a large bowl and rub well into the duck portions. Cover the bowl with some kitchen film and leave in a refrigerator for 8 hours, turning occasionally.

2 Preheat the oven to 220°C/425°F/Gas Mark 7. Drain and reserve the marinade. Place the duck portions, skin side down, in an ovenproof dish. Put in the oven for 30 minutes, basting at least once. Turn the duck portions over, baste and cook for a further 30 minutes, basting at least once. Switch off the oven but leave the duck in it.

3 Spoon 225ml/8fl oz of the marinade into a hot pan, cover and allow to simmer for at least 5 minutes. Strain, whisk in the yogurt and season with salt and black pepper to taste.

4 Serve the duck on a dish garnished with the watercress. The sauce is served in a bowl. If guests are not proficient with chopsticks, the duck should be chopped into bite-sized pieces.

Duck with Ginger Sauce

THIT VIT VÓI XÔT GÙNG

SERVES 4

- **450g/1lb Ho Chi Minh duck**
- **vegetable oil for frying**
- **12 thin slices root ginger, peeled and shredded**
- **22ml/1½ tbsp hot soya paste**
- **22ml/1½ tbsp sweet soya paste or hoisin sauce**
- **8ml/1½ tsp rice wine**
- **22ml/1½ tbsp Nuoc Mam sauce (optional)**
- **1 tsp finely chopped garlic**
- **1 tbsp chilli oil**
- **1 tsp sugar**
- **salt**
- **225ml/8fl oz chicken stock**
- **1 spring onion, shredded**
- **1 red chilli pepper (fresh, shredded, or dried, crumbled)**
- **2 tsp cornflour mixed with a little water**

HO CHI MINH DUCK

- **salt**
- **pinch of five-spice powder**
- **½ tsp finely chopped root ginger**
- **½ tsp finely chopped garlic**
- **½ tsp hot soya paste**
- **1 oven-ready duck (about 1.75–2 kg/4–4½lb)**
- **100ml/4fl oz hot water**
- **45ml/3 tbsp wine vinegar**
- **15g/¾oz sugar**
- **red food colouring**

1 Make the Ho Chi Minh duck by mixing the salt, five-spice powder, ginger, garlic and soya paste. Put the mixture inside the duck's cavity and sew up both ends. Mix the remaining ingredients well and brush over the entire surface with a pastry brush. Leave to dry on a rack with the breast uppermost for 7 hours in a cool, dry place.

2 Preheat the oven to 200°C/400°F/Gas Mark 6. Put the rack together with the duck on a roasting tin and roast for 1 hour. Reduce the heat if the skin begins to burn. (Ideally, the duck should be roasted upright in the Oriental style but most household ovens cannot accommodate an upright duck. Laying it on its back is the next best thing.)

3 Take the cooked duck meat off the bone in as large pieces as possible and cut these into neat pieces about 1 × 2.5cm/½ × 1in. Heat the oil in a wok until it starts smoking and stir-fry the duck pieces for a few minutes. Set these aside making sure to drain well.

4 Empty and wipe the wok, heat some more oil in it and stir-fry the ginger very briskly; add the soya bean pastes, return the duck to the wok and stir in the rice wine, Nuoc Mam sauce, if used, garlic, chilli oil, sugar and salt. Stir-fry for a few more minutes.

5 Add the chicken stock to the wok. As soon as it comes to the boil, reduce the heat and simmer, uncovered, for 5 minutes. Increase the heat, add the spring onions and chilli and cook fast for 1 minute, then stir in the cornflour.

Crispy Roast Duck with Pancakes and Fresh Herbs

THIT VIT QUAY ĂN VỚI BÁNH GIÒ VÀ RAU GIA VI

SERVES 4

- ★ **450g/1lb of Ho Chi Minh duck (see Duck with Ginger Sauce, page 69)**
- ★ **12 wheaten pancakes (these can be obtained from an Asian store or a good delicatessen) or**
- ★ **225g/½lb plain white flour**
- ★ **125g/6oz boiled water**
- ★ **8ml/½ tbsp cold water**
- ★ **5ml/1 tsp sesame seed oil**

VEGETABLE PLATTER

- ★ **1 bunch spring onions, cut into 5cm/2in lengths**
- ★ **50g/2oz fresh coriander**
- ★ **50g/2oz fresh mint**
- ★ **50g/2oz fresh basil**
- ★ **½ cucumber peeled in alternating strips, halved lengthways and sliced thinly crossways**
- ★ **275g/10oz fresh beansprouts**
- ★ **Sweet plum sauce to accompany (this can be obtained from large supermarkets and delicatessens)**

1 To make the pancakes sift the flour into a mixing bowl. Pour in the boiled water, stirring quickly and then stir in the cold water. When cool enough, mould with your hands and form a dough. Cover with a cloth and leave for 30 minutes.

2 When ready, knead lightly on a lightly floured board. Roll the dough into a sausage shape and cut into 2.5cm/1in portions. This will make about 14 rounds. With the heel of the hand flatten into circles of about 6cm/2½in across.

3 Using a pastry brush paint half the pieces with the sesame oil. Place the remaining pieces onto the oiled surfaces making 7 pairs in total. With a lightly floured rolling pin roll out each pair to about 15cm/6in across. Turn them to make them round.

4 Fry for 1–2 minutes in a heavy un-oiled pan until they begin to turn light brown. Turn them over and repeat. They will puff up.

5 Remove and separate the two thin pancakes. Repeat until all the dough is used up. Put on a plate and cover with a cloth to prevent from drying. Steam all the pancakes in a steamer for 7 minutes just before serving with the duck.

6 Arrange the duck on a plate. Arrange the vegetables on a plate. Put some plum sauce into a dish. Place the pancakes on a flat plate. Guests place a teaspoon of plum sauce with some duck and vegetables on a pancake.

Casserole of Duck with Dumplings

VIT TÌM ĂN VÓI BÁNH HÂP

SERVES 4

- ★ **1 duck, about 2.25kg/5lb**
- ★ **1 tsp minced peeled root ginger**
- ★ **salt and black pepper**
- ★ **30ml/2 tbsp dry sherry**
- ★ **4 × 2.5cm/1in slices root ginger, peeled**
- ★ **1 large whole spring onion**
- ★ **100g/4oz sliced ham**
- ★ **225g/8oz can bamboo shoots, cut into 2.5cm/1in pieces**
- ★ **salt**

DUMPLINGS

- ★ **225g/8oz plain flour**
- ★ **225ml/8fl oz boiling water**
- ★ **450g/1lb pork, minced**
- ★ **100g/4oz prawns, peeled and deveined**
- ★ **175g/6oz white cabbage, finely chopped**
- ★ **salt**
- ★ **2 × 2.5cm/1in slices root ginger, peeled minced**
- ★ **1 spring onion, finely chopped**
- ★ **30ml/2 tbsp light soya sauce**
- ★ **30ml/2 tbsp dry sherry**
- ★ **¼ tsp sugar**
- ★ **15ml/1 tbsp sesame oil**
- ★ **1 tbsp cornflour dissolved in 45ml/3 tbsp water**
- ★ **black pepper**
- ★ **plain flour**

1 Remove the fat from the cavity of the duck, discard the parson's nose and trim off any excess neck skin. Rinse and drain the duck. Mix the ginger, salt and black pepper and rub well into the duck, inside and out. Leave to stand for 1 hour.

2 Place the duck in a large casserole, add the sherry, ginger slices and spring onion, cover and bring to a slow boil over moderate heat. Turn down the heat, skim off any scum adding enough liquid so that the duck doesn't burn and adjust the heat so that it simmers at its gentlest. Cover and leave for 3 hours.

3 Make the dumplings by mixing the flour and boiling water in a large bowl, a little at a time, with a wooden spoon. Do not concern yourself with what it looks like at this stage.

4 Chop the pork to loosen it and put it in a second bowl. Slice the prawns lengthways and then cut them into 8mm/¼in pieces. Mix with the pork.

5 Cut the white cabbage leaves lengthways into narrow strips and then cross-cut to dice them. Mince and mix with salt and leave for 5 minutes. Squeeze dry and add to the meat mixture with the rest of the ingredients except the flour. Stir until smooth and pasty. Divide the mixture into 16 portions.

6 Knead the dough for a few minutes until it is soft and smooth, dusting with flour if necessary. Roll it out into a 40cm/16in long sausage and cut with a sharp knife into 2.5cm/1in pieces. Dip the cut sides in flour, press into small round cakes with the palm of your hand and roll out into round wrappers 10cm/4in across.

7 Lay a wrapper in the palm of one hand and put a portion of filling in it with the other. Spread with a table knife to within 1cm/½in of the edge. Gather the wrapper up and press the ends to make a little "basket". Press the back of a knife deep into the basket about 10 times to form indentations, which help to hold the filling in place. You should have 16 dumplings. Put them on a plate and steam over a medium-high heat for 20 minutes. Set aside.

8 Skim off the fat from the casserole after it has been cooking for 3 hours and discard it. Scatter in the ham, bamboo shoots and the dumplings. Cover and simmer for another 5–10 minutes. Add salt to taste.

9 Serve in the casserole. Guests help themselves by tearing the bird apart with chopsticks. If they are not sufficiently proficient, you could chop it in the kitchen, put the pieces back into the casserole and bring it back to the boil before serving at the table. Ladle into individual soup bowls.

Marinated Quail in Honey

CHIM CÚT UÓP VÓI MÂT ONG

SERVES 4

- **1 tsp coriander seeds, lightly crushed**
- **2 tbsp clear honey**
- **2 onions, sliced**
- **300ml/½ pt dry cider**
- **300ml/½ pt chilli vinegar**
- **8 quails**
- **25g/1oz butter**
- **30ml/2 tbsp vegetable oil**
- **salt and freshly ground black pepper**
- **chopped parsley to garnish**

1 Mix the coriander, honey, onion, cider and vinegar in a large bowl (not a metal one). Add the quails and marinate overnight.

2 Preheat the oven to 180°C/350°F/Gas Mark 4. Drain and reserve the marinade. Dry the quails with absorbent kitchen paper. Heat the butter and oil in a large casserole. Add the quails, 4 at a time, seasoning them with salt and black pepper. Brown on both sides.

3 Put all the birds in the casserole and pour the marinade over them. Cover and cook in the oven for 40–45 minutes, basting occasionally, or until tender. Garnish with chopped parsley to serve.

Braised Quails' Eggs with Bean Curd and Vegetables

RAU VÀ DÂU PHU TRÔN TRUNG

SERVES 4

This recipe was given to me by the respected and longstanding chef of the Mekong of Pimlico, London.

- **1 piece bean curd, cut into 6 pieces 1cm/½in thick**
- **90ml/6 tbsp vegetable oil**
- **10 straw mushrooms or firm button mushrooms**
- **8 quails' eggs, hard-boiled and shelled**
- **1 spring onion, cut into 2.5cm/1in lengths**
- **2 pieces canned bamboo shoots, cut into 2.5cm/1in cubes**
- **20ml/4 tsp bottled saté sauce**
- **1 tsp cornflour**
- **15ml/3 tsp Nuoc Mam sauce or light soya sauce**
- **2 tsp sugar**
- **100ml/4fl oz water**

1 Fry the bean curd in 60ml/4 tbsp hot oil until brown, taking care not to let it stick. Set aside and discard the oil.

2 Put the remaining oil into a small casserole dish with a tight-fitting lid. Heat over a medium heat. Add the straw mushrooms, quails' eggs, spring onion, bean curd, bamboo shoots and saté sauce.

3 Mix the cornflour, Nuoc Mam sauce and sugar to form a smooth paste. Mix into the water. Stir this into the casserole pot and cover. Cook for 4 minutes.

Fried Frogs' Legs with Garlic Sauce

CHÂN ÊCH CHIÊN VÓI XÔT TOI

SERVES 4

- **4 pairs jumbo frogs' legs (about 450g/1lb), trimmed**
- **1 stalk fresh lemon grass, soaked for 1 hour in warm water and finely chopped or 1 tbsp dried lemon grass**
- **2 fresh red chilli peppers, sliced**
- **2 spring onions, sliced**
- **2 cloves garlic, crushed**
- **1½ tsp sugar**
- **salt**
- **30ml/2 tbsp Nuoc Mam sauce or 30ml/2 tbsp Maggi seasoning and 1 garlic clove, crushed**
- **50g/2oz bean thread vermicelli**
- **30ml/2 tbsp vegetable oil**
- **1 small onion, chopped**
- **225ml/8fl oz chicken stock or water**
- **100ml/4fl oz coconut cream or double cream**
- **3 tsp cornflour mixed with a little water**
- **freshly ground black pepper**
- **coriander sprigs to garnish**

1 Chop the frogs' legs into bite-sized pieces and rinse with cold water to get rid of any pieces of bone. Pat dry and put in the refrigerator.

2 Combine the lemon grass, chillies, spring onion, garlic, sugar, salt and 15ml/1 tbsp Nuoc Mam sauce in a blender or food procesor until a very fine paste results. Rub the paste over the frogs' legs, cover and refrigerate again for 30 minutes.

3 Soak the vermicelli in warm water for 30 minutes. Drain and cut into 5cm/2in lengths.

4 Heat the oil in a wok over moderate heat. Add the onion and sauté until soft, then add the frogs' legs and brown well, turning them over from time to time. This should take 3 minutes. Add the chicken stock and bring to the boil. Reduce the heat, cover and simmer for 15 minutes.

5 Uncover the wok and add the coconut cream. Add the cornflour and the remaining Nuoc Mam sauce. Stir as the sauce thickens and cook for another 15 minutes.

6 Add the vermicelli and bring to the boil. Remove from the heat. Sprinkle with black pepper and garnish with coriander sprigs.

7 Serve immediately with rice or French bread or rice noodles. It is advisable to offer an alternative to frogs' legs since there are a few cynics who do not believe that frogs' legs taste very much like chicken.

Fried Frogs' Legs with Garlic Sauce ▶

Fried Frogs' Legs with Banana

CHÂN ÊCH CHIÊN ĂN VÓI CHUÔI

SERVES 4

- **8 pairs frogs' legs**
- **45ml/3 tbsp peanut oil**
- **2 cloves of garlic, crushed**
- **15ml/1 tbsp dry sherry**
- **15ml/1 tbsp Nuoc Mam sauce or light soya sauce**
- **cornflour**
- **vegetable oil for frying**
- **1 green sweet pepper, cut into strips**
- **1 red chilli, chopped**

BANANA BATTER

- **50g/2oz self-raising flour**
- **150g/5oz plain flour**
- **salt**
- **¼ tsp baking powder**
- **1 egg white, beaten until stiff**
- **vegetable oil**
- **4 bananas**

1 Place the whole frogs' legs in a bowl. Mix in 30ml/2 tbsp peanut oil, garlic, sherry and Nuoc Mam sauce. Sprinkle with some cornflour and mix well. Place in the refrigerator and leave to marinade for at least 2 hours.

2 Heat the vegetable oil in a large pan and deep-fry the legs for about 5 minutes. Take care not to burn.

3 In another wok or pan, heat the remaining peanut oil. Add the pepper and chilli. Quickly toss the legs into the pepper and chilli, stir thoroughly then remove.

4 To make the banana batter, sieve the flour with the salt and baking powder. Stir in enough water to form a liquidy paste. Lightly fold in the beaten egg white.

5 Heat 7.5cm/3in oil in a wok. Peel the bananas, cut in half lengthways and dunk into the batter. Dip them into the hot oil and cook in batches until golden and puffy. Drain on absorbent kitchen paper and serve with the frogs' legs.

Pork Dishes

Steamed Minced Pork with Saltfish

THIT LON XAY HÂP VÓI CÁ MUÔI

SERVES 4

- **50g/2oz saltfish**
- **1 tbsp Nuoc Mam sauce or light soya sauce**
- **1 tsp sugar**
- **450g/1lb lean pork, minced**
- **15ml/1 tbsp sesame oil**

SEASONINGS

- **1 tbsp minced spring onions (white part only)**
- **15ml/1 tbsp dark soya sauce**
- **10ml/2 tsp rice wine or dry sherry**
- **½ tsp sugar**
- **salt and freshly ground black pepper**
- **15ml/1 tbsp sesame oil**
- **1 egg, well beaten**
- **1 tbsp cornflour**
- **2 level tbsp plain flour**

1 Soak the saltfish overnight, taking care to change the water at least once. Strip off the dark skin and discard. Shred the saltfish, rinse and squeeze dry. Chop it roughly and put it in a mixing bowl with the Nuoc Mam sauce and sugar, stir and then set aside.

2 Chop the minced pork until it is smooth. Scoop into a mixing bowl and add the spring onions, soya sauce, rice wine, sugar, salt and black pepper and sesame oil. Blend thoroughly. Add the beaten egg, a little at a time, mixing all the while. Sprinkle in the cornflour and plain flour, stirring them into the mixture until absolutely smooth. Divide into 16 portions.

3 Squeeze the saltfish to remove excess moisture. Add 15ml/1 tbsp sesame oil and mix thoroughly. Divide into 16 portions.

4 Grease your palms with oil and place one portion of meat in the palm of one hand. Flatten with the fingers of the other hand. Put a portion of saltfish in the centre and fold the meat over it. Roll lightly into a ball. Make 16 balls.

5 Steam the balls over a high heat for at least 15 minutes and transfer them to a serving dish with the meat juices. Delightful.

Minced Pork, Prawn and Pineapple Salad with a Fish Sauce Dressing

THIT LON, TÔM XAY TRÔN DÚA ĂN VÓI NUÓC XÔT CÀ

SERVES 4

- **450g/1lb fresh lean pork, minced or, preferably, finely chopped**
- **30ml/2 tbsp water**
- **225g/8oz cooked prawns**
- **30ml/2 tbsp lemon juice**
- **30ml/2 tbsp Nuoc Mam sauce, or 15ml/1 tbsp light soya sauce 15ml/1 tbsp Maggi seasoning and 3ml/½ tsp anchovy essence**
- **½ tsp dried powdered chilli**
- **1 tsp fresh red chilli pepper, finely sliced**
- **2 tbsp onion, finely sliced**
- **2 tbsp spring onions, cut into 1cm/½in sections**
- **2 tbsp roasted peanuts**
- **2 slices pineapple, roughly chopped**
- **2 tbsp ginger root, finely sliced**
- **1 tbsp fresh mint leaves, chopped**
- **2 tbsp fresh coriander leaves and stem, chopped**
- **6 large lettuce leaves**

GARNISH

- **roasted peanuts**
- **1 tbsp finely sliced root ginger**
- **pinch of dried powdered chilli**
- **fresh red sliced chilli pepper**
- **sprigs of mint**
- **springs of coriander**
- **spring onion curls (see page 14)**
- **chilli flowers (see page 16)**

Temples abound in Vietnam, and are regularly frequented.

1 Cook the pork in a wok over medium heat with the water until the pork is cooked thoroughly but still tender and juicy. Remove from the heat.

2 Add the prawns, lemon juice, Nuoc Mam sauce, and dried and fresh chilli and stir. Add the onion, spring onions, peanuts, pineapple, ginger, mint and coriander leaves. Toss lightly.

3 Serve on a bed of lettuce leaves. Garnish with peanuts, ginger, chilli, sprigs of mint and coriander, spring onion curls and chilli flowers.

Vietnamese Pork au Caramel

THIT LON NÂU CA-RA-MEN KIÊU VIÊT NAM

SERVES 4

- **50g/2oz sugar**
- **30ml/2 tbsp water**
- **450g/1lb leg of pork, cut into large cubes**
- **3 daikon (white Chinese radishes), peeled and thinly sliced**
- **½ onion, chopped**
- **75ml/3fl oz Nuoc Mam sauce or light soya sauce**
- **freshly ground black pepper**

1 Put the sugar in the wok and heat gently until it starts to smell as though it is burning. Stir in the water very carefully so that the mixture does not break up.

2 Add the pork and radishes and cover with water. Add the remaining ingredients and bring to the boil. Reduce the heat, cover and allow to simmer for about an hour or until the pork is cooked.

Pig Trotter Stew

CHÂN MÓNG LON HÂM

SERVES 4

- **1kg/2lb pigs' trotters, washed, blanched and chopped into 4–5cm/1½–2in pieces**
- **1.2 litres/2 pt chicken or pork stock**
- **1 large onion, sliced**
- **3 boiled potatoes, quartered**
- **3 tomatoes, diced**
- **50g/2oz green beans or similar vegetable, sliced**
- **3 tbsp beansprouts**

VIETNAMESE BOUQUET GARNI

- **2 large celery sticks with leaves, roughly chopped**
- **6 small coriander plants with roots, roughly chopped**
- **2 large stalks lemon grass, chopped**
- **6 large cloves garlic, finely chopped**
- **1 cinnamon stick**
- **2 star anise**
- **1 tbsp black peppercorns**

TO GARNISH

- **3 tbsp fresh coriander, chopped**
- **3 tbsp spring onion, chopped**

1 Put the trotters in a large saucepan and bring to the boil. Allow to boil for about 20–30 minutes until the meat pulls away from the bones. Drain.

2 Put the trotters back into the washed saucepan and add the stock and a little extra water if necessary to cover the meat. Bring to the boil. Wrap the bouquet garni in a piece of cloth and tie to form a little bundle. Drop this into the saucepan when it starts to boil. Simmer for 10 minutes or so until you get the right consistency, which should be slightly thickened.

3 Add the onion, potatoes and tomatoes and simmer for a little white, just long enough for them to get warmed through but not long enough for them to disintegrate. Just before serving, add the beans and cook until they are just tender.

4 Remove the bouquet garni and stir in the beansprouts. Sprinkle the garnish over the stew.

Grilled Pigs' Trotters

CHÂN MÓNG LON NUÓNG

SERVES 4

- **4 tbsp fermented black beans, soaked in cold water for 6 minutes and drained**
- **5cm/2in root ginger, peeled and chopped**
- **4 cloves garlic, chopped**
- **2 large red chilli peppers, chopped or ½ tsp chilli powder**
- **2 tsp brown sugar**
- **15ml/1 tbsp Nuoc Mam sauce or 15ml/1 tbsp ligh soya sauce and 3ml/1 tsp anchovy essence**
- **30ml/2 tbsp lemon juice**
- **30ml/2 tbsp peanut oil**
- **30ml/2 tbsp water**
- **1kg/2lb pigs' trotters, washed, blanched and chopped into 4–5cm/1½–2in pieces**

1 Put all the ingredients except the trotters into a blender or food processor and blend until smooth. Empty into a large bowl and add the trotters. Mix until the trotters are thoroughly coated and leave in the refrigerator for at least 2 hours, overnight if possible.

2 Put the trotters in a dish that will fit the steamer and steam for 1½ hours or until the trotters are tender. (If you don't have a steamer, use the largest saucepan you have. Turn a fair-sized bowl upside and and place it in the bottom. Put the bowl containing the trotters on top of this and add water halfway up the bowl containing the trotters.)

3 Drain the meat and reserve the cooking juice. Grill the trotters until they are just crisp on the outside, brushing with the reserved cooking juice.

Rickshaws – cheap and comfortable – are the most common form of transport.

Stuffed Roast Suckling Pig

HEO SUA QUAY CÓ DÔN

SERVES 20

- **4.5kg/10lb prepared suckling pig (ask your butcher to leave enough flesh and skin on the belly for sewing)**
- **juice of 1 lime**
- **2 tbsp tea salt**
- **4 cloves, ground**
- **freshly ground black pepper**
- **vegetable oil**

STUFFING

- **heart, liver and kidneys of the pig**
- **20g/3¼oz butter**
- **2 onions, finely chopped**
- **4 cloves garlic, finely chopped**
- **350g/12oz fresh breadcrumbs**
- **1 red chilli pepper, chopped**
- **4 tbsp chopped spring onions**
- **1 large sprig of parsley, finely chopped**
- **15ml/1 tbsp Nuoc Mam sauce or light soya sauce**
- **175ml/6oz rice wine**
- **½ tsp thyme, finely chopped**
- **½ tsp allspice, crushed**
- **juice of 1 lime**
- **salt**

SAUCE

- **600ml/1 pt chicken stock**
- **600ml/1 pt clear honey**
- **120ml/4½oz light soya sauce**
- **60ml/4 tbsp tomato purée**
- **4 tsp five-spice powder**
- **100ml/4fl oz rice wine or sherry**
- **salt**
- **2 tbsp cornflour mixed with a little water**

1 Run cold water over the suckling pig and dry thoroughly inside and out. Rub the inside of the pig with lime juice. Mix the salt, cloves and black pepper and use half of it to rub the inside of the pig.

2 Clean and wash the liver, heart and kidney. Dry and mince. Melt the butter in a pan on a low heat, add the onions and garlic and sauté until softened. Add the minced liver, heart and kidney mixture and continue to sauté for a further 5 minutes. Remove from heat and allow to cool.

3 Add the other ingredients, mixing well. (If the stuffing is too dry, add 15–30ml/1–2 tbsp water or milk.) Fill the cavity with the stuffing and sew it up with kitchen twine. Stuff a ball of foil in the pig's mouth. Tie each pair of legs together and fold under the animal. Place belly downwards in a shallow pan. Brush the back with oil and sprinkle the remainder of the ground cloves, sea salt and black pepper over the suckling pig. Cover the ears with foil for the first 90 minutes of cooking.

4 Preheat the oven to 170°C/325°F/Gas Mark 3 and cook the pig for 2½ hours or until the juices run clear when pricked with a knife, basting regularly. Remove from the pan and allow to cool for 15 minutes. Replace the foil in the mouth with an orange and put the pig on a serving dish.

5 Drain the juices from the roasting pan to a wok. Add all the sauce ingredients except the cornflour. Bring the juices to the boil and add the cornflour, stirring gently until it thickens.

Pork Knuckle and Peanut Stew

KHUY CHÂN LON HAM VOI LAC

SERVES 4

- **3 fresh pork knuckles**
- **1 smoked pork knuckle or ham hock**
- **30g/1½oz fresh peanuts, blanched**
- **4 × 2.5cm/1in slices peeled ginger, 1cm/½in thick**
- **2 large spring onions**
- **2.8 litres/5 pt water**
- **salt**

1 Put the fresh and smoked knuckles, peanuts, ginger and spring onions into a large, heavy pot together with the water and bring to the boil over a high heat. Turn down the heat to a simmer and skim off any scum. Cover and simmer for 2½ hours, stirring once in a while.

2 Skim off scum and season with salt to taste. Discard the ginger, spring onions and the knuckle bones, if so desired. The meat may be served in chunks or cut into small pieces. Serve hot with a dip of Nuoc Mam sauce with a sprinkling of ground Szechuan peppercorns.

Stir-fried Pork Slices and Celery

THIT LON XÀO VÓI CÂN TÂY

SERVES 4

- ★ **30ml/2 tbsp vegetable oil**
- ★ **450g/1lb lean pork, sliced thinly and cut in 2.5 × 4cm/ 1½in pieces**
- ★ **5ml/1 tsp soya sauce**
- ★ **1 tsp sugar**
- ★ **225g/8oz button mushrooms**
- ★ **225g/8oz spring cabbage, cut in 5cm/2in slices with tougher stalks discarded**
- ★ **4 celery sticks, sliced thinly**
- ★ **15ml/1 tbsp Nuoc Mam sauce (optional)**
- ★ **45ml/3 tbsp chicken stock**
- ★ **cornflour**
- ★ **salt**

1 Heat 15ml/1 tbsp oil in the wok, add the pork and stir-fry over highest heat for 2½ minutes or longer if the pork needs more cooking. Add the soya sauce and sugar and stir with the pork for a further 2 minutes. Scoop into a bowl and keep in a warm oven.

2 Wipe the wok and pour in the remaining oil. Add the mushrooms, cabbage and celery and stir-fry for 1½ minutes. Add the Nuoc Mam sauce, if using, and stock and stir-fry for another minute. Cover and leave to cook for a further 2 minutes. Then add the cooked sliced pork with the cornflour and salt to taste. Stir and mix thoroughly for a minute or so and serve immediately with rice or noodles.

Steamed Minced Pork and Aubergine

THIT LON XAY HẤP VỚI CÀ TÍM

SERVES 4

- **1 aubergine, about 350g/12oz**
- **salt and freshly ground black pepper**
- **½ tsp vegetable oil**
- **1 small onion, thinly sliced and then coarsely chopped**
- **1 egg, lightly beaten**
- **450g/1lb minced pork**
- **1 tbsp chopped gherkin or pickles**
- **1 tsp sugar**
- **30ml/2 tbsp Nuoc Mam sauce or light soya sauce**
- **1 tbsp cornflour**
- **15ml/1 tbsp rice wine or dry sherry**

1 Peel the aubergine, slice it into pieces about 1cm/½in thick and then chop into 2.5cm/1in pieces. Sprinkle and rub with salt and pepper and a little oil.

2 Mix the onion, egg, pork, gherkin, sugar, Nuoc Mam sauce, cornflour, rice wine and a little salt. Mix with a wooden spoon until the ingredients are thoroughly mixed.

3 Place the aubergine pieces at the bottom of a bowl and pack the pork mixture on top of the aubergine so that no vegetable shows above the surface.

4 Place the bowl in a steamer over the wok and steam vigorously for 45 minutes. If you don't have a steamer, use the largest saucepan you have. Turn a fair-sized bowl upside down and place it in the bottom. Put the bowl containing the pork and aubergine on top of this and add water to halfway up the bowl containing the pork and aubergine. Serve hot. A stir-fried dish is an ideal accompaniment.

Spicy Grilled Pork on a Bed of Vermicelli

THIT BÒ THIT LON NUÓNG VÓI GIA VI ĂN VÓI BÚN

SERVES 4

- **225g/8oz rice vermicelli**
- **450g/1lb fresh belly pork with skin, cut against the grain into 8mm/¼in strips, about 5cm/2in long**
- **450g/1lb beef, minced**
- **8 cloves garlic, minced**

CARAMEL SAUCE

- **100g/4oz sugar**
- **50ml/2fl oz Nuoc Mam sauce, or Maggi sauce and ½ tsp anchovy essence, mixed thoroughly**
- **4 spring onions, thinly sliced**
- **freshly ground black pepper**

1 Soak the vermicelli in warm water until soft. Drain and set aside.

2 Make the caramel sauce by swirling the sugar gently in a wok over a hot heat. Be careful not to let the sugar blacken but ignore the smoke. Remove from the heat and add the Nuoc Mam sauce or Maggi substitute. Return to a low heat and gently boil until the sugar dissolves. Add the spring onions and pepper and stir.

3 Put 24 bamboo skewers into water and allow to soak for at least 30 minutes.

4 Meanwhile, put the pork and beef into two separate bowls. Put the garlic and half of the caramel sauce onto the beef. Put the remainder of the caramel sauce onto the pork. Blend both with the hand and allow to stand for 30 minutes. Make 24 meatballs out of the beef.

5 Skewer the beef balls and pork slices and cook under a hot grill for 15–20 minutes turning frequently. Place on the bed of vermicelli. Serve with a Vegetable Platter (see Crispy Roast Duck with Pancakes and Fresh Herbs, page 70).

Beef Dishes

Beef in Coconut Milk

THIT BÒ NAU VOI NUOC DÙA

SERVES 4

This ever-popular and traditional Vietnamese dish was kindly given to me by Madame Binh of Thanh Binh, London.

- **30ml/2 tbsp vegetable oil**
- **1 clove garlic, crushed**
- **225g/8oz topside of beef, thinly sliced**
- **1 small onion, thinly sliced**
- **pinch of turmeric**
- **½ green chilli pepper,**
- **1cm/½in lemon grass, cut from the bottom, thinly sliced**
- **15ml/1 tbsp canned coconut milk**

GARNISH

- **1 tbsp peanuts, crushed**
- **handful of fresh coriander, chopped**

1 Heat the oil until very hot. Add the garlic. When the smell is released, add everything except the coconut milk. Stir-fry for about 3 minutes or until the meat is cooked.

2 Add the coconut milk and stir once. Serve garnished with crushed peanuts and chopped coriander.

Spicy Beef Stew

THIT BO HÂM GIA VI

SERVES 4

This particular stew is, arguably, Vietnam's boeuf à la bourguignonne. *This is my father's recipe, but there are several versions of the same dish. I was very fond of it as a child; I still am.*

- ★ **45ml/3 tbsp vegetable oil**
- ★ **2 medium onions, finely chopped**
- ★ **5 cloves garlic, finely chopped**
- ★ **10 spring onions, dead skin peeled off**
- ★ **1 stalk lemon grass, cut into 5cm/2in sections and crushed**
- ★ **1kg/2lb stewing beef, cut into 2.5cm/1in cubes**
- ★ **1.2 litres/2 pt water**
- ★ **90ml/3½fl oz yellow bean sauce, chopped and crushed**
- ★ **1 tsp chilli powder**
- ★ **4 star anise**
- ★ **2.5cm/1in cinnamon stick**
- ★ **½ tsp whole peppercorns**
- ★ **sugar**

1 Heat 15ml/1 tbsp oil in a wok over a medium high heat. Put in the onions, garlic and whole spring onions and stir-fry for 2 minutes. Add the lemon grass and continue to stir until the onions become lightly brown, remove the spring onions and set aside.

2 Heat the remaining oil over a high heat. Stir-fry as many pieces of beef as are convenient until they are brown, turning them over from time to time. Continue until all the beef has been cooked.

3 Add the water. Add the lemon grass mixture, yellow bean sauce, chilli powder, star anise, cinnamon, peppercorns and sugar and bring to the boil. Cover and lower the heat to simmer gently for 1½ hours.

4 Add the reserved spring onions; cover again and allow to simmer for a further 15 minutes or until the sauce has thickened a little and the meat is tender.

Spicy Beef Stew ▶

Spicy Beef Stew II

THIT BO HÂM GIA VI

SERVES 4

- ★ **1kg/2lb stewing beef, cut into 5cm/2in cubes**
- ★ **2 stalks lemon grass, sliced paper-thin and finely chopped**
- ★ **2 fresh red chilli peppers, minced**
- ★ **2 tsp sugar**
- ★ **2 tbsp fresh ginger, grated**
- ★ **2 tsp ground cinnamon**
- ★ **2 tsp curry powder**
- ★ **45ml/3 tbsp Nuoc Mam sauce or 45ml/3 tbsp light soya sauce and 3ml/½ tsp anchovy essence**
- ★ **salt and freshly ground black pepper**
- ★ **65ml/4½ tbsp vegetable oil**
- ★ **1 large onion, minced**
- ★ **6 cloves garlic, minced**
- ★ **100ml/4fl oz tomato purée**
- ★ **4 star anise**
- ★ **1.2 litres/2 pt water**
- ★ **2 medium carrots, cut into 2.5cm/1in chunks**
- ★ **2 medium potatoes, peeled and cut into 2.5cm/1in chunks**
- ★ **1 small daikon (white Chinese radish), peeled and cut into 2.5cm/1in chunks**

1 Mix the beef, lemon grass, chillies, sugar, ginger, cinnamon, curry powder, Nuoc Mam sauce, salt and black pepper and leave to stand for 1 hour.

2 Heat 4 tbsp oil in the wok over a high heat. Add the beef and marinade and stir quickly to sear. This should not take much more than 2 minutes. Remove the meat to a bowl and set aside.

3 Add a little more oil and, when hot, add the onion and garlic and stir-fry until fragrant. Add the tomato purée and stir for 2 minutes. Add the beef, star anise, a little salt and the water. Bring the mixture to the boil, reduce the heat to low, cover the wok and simmer until the beef is tender – about 1½ hours.

4 Add the carrots and simmer for 10 minutes. Add the potatoes and simmer for a further 10 minutes. Finally, add the daikon and cook for another 10 minutes.

Beef with Lemon Grass and Mushrooms

THIT BÒ NÂU VÓI SA VÀ NÂM

SERVES 4

- **450g/1lb fillet steak, sliced very thinly across the grain and cut into 5 × 7.5cm/2 × 3in pieces**
- **2 stalks fresh lemon grass, sliced paper-thin and finely chopped**
- **2 fresh red chilli peppers, minced**
- **6 cloves garlic, minced**
- **45ml/3 tbsp Nuoc Mam sauce or light soya sauce**
- **1 tsp arrowroot or cornflour**
- **freshly ground black pepper**
- **50ml/3½ tbsp vegetable oil**
- **2 medium onions, finely sliced**
- **100g/4oz button mushrooms**
- **1 tsp sugar**
- **50g/2oz roasted peanuts, coarsely ground**
- **sprigs of coriander to garnish**

1 Combine the beef, lemon grass, chilli, half the garlic, 30ml/2 tbsp Nuoc Mam sauce, arrowroot, black pepper and 30ml/2 tbsp oil in a bowl. Set aside for 30 minutes.

2 Pour 1 tbsp oil in the wok over a medium heat and add the onions and the remaining garlic. Stir-fry for 1–2 minutes until they are golden brown. Remove the onions and set aside. Add 8ml/½ tbsp more oil and, when hot, add the beef, the mushrooms, the rest of the Nuoc Mam sauce and the sugar. Sauté over a high heat for 1–2 minutes or until the beef is just cooked.

3 Scoop the food from the wok and arrange it on a warmed serving dish. Arrange the sautéed onions around it and sprinkle the peanuts and black pepper over everything. Garnish with coriander sprigs.

French Colonial Steak

BIP-TECH KIÊU PHÁP THUÔC DIA

SERVES 4

- **30ml/2 tbsp chilli sauce**
- **2 cloves garlic, crushed**
- **30ml/2 tbsp black vinegar**
- **1 piece of entrecôte or fillet steak, about 1kg/2lb in weight**

GARNISH

- **1 shallot, thinly sliced and deep-fried until crisp**
- **1 tbsp chopped peanuts**

1 Mix the chilli sauce, garlic and vinegar in a bowl. Cover the steak with this marinade and leave overnight if possible.

2 Set the grill at its highest. Slip the steak under it for a good 4 minutes on each side and allow it to rest for 5 minutes.

3 Cut the steak across the grain in thin slices and place attractively on a serving dish. Sprinkle with the shallots and peanuts.

Fresh produce abounds in Vietnam – here a colourful display of carrots, onions and potatoes.

Stir-fried Beef with Peppers and Bamboo Shoots

THIT BÒ XÀO NHANH VỚI MĂNG VÀ ỚT NGOT

SERVES 4

- **15ml/1 tbsp vegetable oil**
- **450g/1lb rump steak, thinly sliced**
- **3 spring onions, cut in 1cm/½in lengths**
- **2 cloves garlic, crushed**
- **100g/4oz canned bamboo shoots, sliced**
- **1 large green sweet pepper, seeded and sliced**
- **30ml/2 tbsp Nuoc Mam sauce or 30ml/2 tbsp light soya sauce and ½ tsp anchovy essence**
- **150ml/¼ pt beef stock**
- **25g/1oz sugar**
- **2 tsp cornflour mixed with a little water**

1 Heat the oil in a wok over a high heat, add the beef and stir-fry for 2–3 minutes, stirring all the while, to seal in the flavours of the meat. Scoop out the beef and place it in a warm oven.

2 Add the spring onions and garlic to the wok and stir-fry over a moderate heat for 3 minutes. Increase the heat to high, stir in the bamboo shoots and pepper and stir-fry for 1–2 minutes.

3 Stir in the Nuoc Mam sauce, stock and sugar. Cover and cook for 3 minutes. Return the beef to the wok and stir for 1 minute. Add the cornflour to the beef mixture and stir constantly until the mixture thickens. Serve immediately.

Crispy Beef Slices Served with a Spicy Dip

THIT BÒ CÁT LÁT GIÒN ĂN VÓI NUÓC CHÂM

SERVES 4

- **450g/1lb fillet steak, cut across the grain into thin slices 5cm/2in long**
- **2 eggs, beaten**
- **15ml/1 tbsp sesame seed oil**
- **15ml/1 tbsp Nuoc Mam sauce (optional)**
- **¼ tsp sugar**
- **2 tsp root ginger, finely minced**
- **5ml/1 tsp rice wine or dry sherry**
- **vegetable oil for deep frying**
- **salt and freshly ground black pepper**
- **cornflour**

DIP

- **60ml/4 tbsp Nuoc Mam sauce, or light soya sauce**
- **10ml/2 tsp chilli oil**

1 Mix the dip ingredients thoroughly in a bowl and set aside.

2 Mix all the other ingredients except the cornflour in a second bowl and allow to marinate for 1 hour before cooking.

3 Dredge the beef slices in cornflour. In a wok, deep-fry a few pieces at a time until golden brown. The colour comes from the cornflour and not the beef. Drain, and put on a dish and serve with the chilli dip.

Beef and French Fries

THIT BÒ VÀ KHOAI TÂY CHIÊN

SERVES 4

This recipe was given to me by the chef of the very French-influenced Bonjour Vietnam Restaurant, London. As in Vietnam, it is eaten with chunks of French bread.

- **120ml/8 tbsp vegetable oil**
- **2 large potatoes, peeled and cut into matchsticks**
- **1 medium onion, thinly sliced**
- **2 cloves garlic, minced**
- **275g/10oz sirloin steak, cut into thin slices**
- **10ml/2 tsp cornflour**
- **15ml/3 tsp water**
- **1 tsp sugar**
- **10 ml/2 tsp Nuoc Mam sauce or light soya sauce**

1 Pour 90ml/6 tbsp oil into a frying pan. Add the potatoes and fry until brown. Discard the oil and set aside the potatoes.

2 Fry the onion and garlic in 30ml/2 tbsp oil. Add the beef and stir-fry for 1 minute.

3 Mix the cornflour, water, sugar and Nuoc Mam sauce to a smooth paste. Add this to the beef and stir. Add the potatoes and stir well to combine.

LAMB DISHES

Sautéed Lamb with Aubergine in a Sauce

THIT CÙU XÔT-TÊ ĂN VÓI CÁ TÍM VÀ XÔT

SERVES 4

- **2 large aubergines, ends cut off, thickly sliced**
- **45ml/3 tbsp olive oil**
- **8 lamb cutlets, trimmed**
- **2 cloves garlic, crushed**
- **6 large tomatoes, blanched, skinned and thickly sliced**
- **salt and freshly ground black pepper**

SAUCE

- **2 tbsp fresh mint, chopped**
- **150ml/¼ pt natural yogurt**
- **freshly ground black pepper**

GARNISH

- **1 lemon, sliced**
- **sprigs of mint**

1 Sprinkle salt over the aubergine and leave for 20 minutes. Rinse the aubergine and dry with absorbent kitchen paper.

2 Heat 30ml/2 tbsp olive oil in a wok over a very high heat and add the lamb cutlets. When brown, lower the heat and continue cooking until the meat is tender – about 5 minutes on each side. Remove from the wok, drain on absorbent kitchen paper and keep in a warm oven.

3 Add the remaining oil to the wok and fry the aubergine slices with the garlic until they are lightly browned on both sides. (If the oil dries out, add a little more.) When they are cooked, push them up the side of the wok and add the tomato slices. Stir-fry for a few moments and season with salt and pepper.

4 Place the vegetables on a dish and arrange the cutlets over the vegetables. Garnish with lemon slices and sprigs of mint.

5 Prepare the sauce by stirring the mint into the yogurt. Grind some black pepper over it and serve in a small bowl.

Lamb in a Hot Garlic Sauce

THIT CÙU ĂN VÓI XÔT TOI ÓT

SERVES 4

- ★ 225g/8oz spinach or any green vegetable
- ★ 30ml/2 tbsp vegetable oil
- ★ 225g/8oz lean lamb, thinly sliced
- ★ 4 cloves garlic, finely chopped
- ★ freshly ground white pepper
- ★ ½ tsp sugar
- ★ 15ml/1 tbsp Nuoc Mam sauce or 15ml/1 tbsp light soya sauce and 3ml/1 tsp anchovy essence
- ★ 15ml/1 tbsp oyster sauce
- ★ fresh sprigs of mint and/or coriander to garnish

1 Blanch the greens in boiling water for 1 minute. Drain and place on a serving dish.

2 Heat the oil in a wok and stir-fry the lamb until nearly cooked. This should not take more than 2 minutes. Add the garlic, pepper, sugar, Nuoc Mam sauce and oyster sauce and stir-fry until the lamb is completely cooked and tender.

3 Pour the lamb and sauce over the greens. Garnish with mint and/or coriander sprigs.

Lamb in Hot Garlic Sauce ▶

Lamb's Liver with Ginger and Coriander

GAN CÙU VÓI GÙNG VÀ NGÒ

SERVES 4

- ★ 450g/1lb lamb's liver, cut into 4cm/1½in wide strips and cut again crossways into strips 5mm/⅛in thick
- ★ 30ml/2 tbsp vegetable oil
- ★ 1 large onion, cut into wedges about 4cm/1½in wide
- ★ 2 medium green sweet peppers, halved
- ★ salt
- ★ 15ml/1 tbsp sesame oil

SAUCE

- ★ 30ml/2 tbsp Nuoc Mam sauce or light soya sauce
- ★ 30ml/2 tbsp rice wine or dry sherry
- ★ 10ml/2 tsp sugar
- ★ 2 large cloves garlic, coarsely chopped
- ★ 1 tbsp fermented black beans, rinsed and coarsely chopped
- ★ 2 × 2.5cm/1in slices root ginger, peeled and minced
- ★ 1 tbsp fresh coriander, chopped
- ★ 1 spring onion, coarsely chopped
- ★ 10ml/2 tsp cornflour mixed with 30ml/2 tbsp water

1 Bring a large saucepan half full of water to the boil. Put in the liver slices and stir until the water begins to puff into a boil again. Drain the liver and hold under the cold water tap to stop the cooking. Drain and set aside.

2 Combine the Nuoc Mam sauce, rice wine and sugar and stir until the sugar dissolves.

3 Heat a wok over high heat and add 15ml/1 tbsp oil. Scatter in the onions and peppers and stir and toss vigorously until they are shining. Sprinkle in some salt and stir for about 1 minute until the onions are translucent. Transfer to a dish.

4 Wipe the wok, add the remaining oil and put in the garlic, black beans, ginger, coriander and spring onions and stir for about 30 seconds to sear them. Add the liver and stir for a further 30 seconds.

5 Add the Nuoc Mam mixture and toss and turn the meat. Add the cooked vegetables and stir them around so they integrate with the meat. Add the cornflour to the wok, a little at a time, stirring constantly. Sprinkle in the sesame oil, toss a couple of times, and ladle out on a hot serving dish.

Stir-fried Lamb with Mint and Chilli

THIT CÙU XÀO VÓI RAU THOM VÀ ÓT

SERVES 4

- **20ml/1½ tbsp vegetable oil**
- **225g/8oz lean lamb, cut in fine strips**
- **1 clove garlic, finely chopped**
- **15ml/1 tbsp oyster sauce**
- **15ml/1 tbsp Nuoc Mam sauce or 15ml/1 tbsp Maggi liquid seasoning and 3ml/½ tsp anchovy essence**
- **pinch of sugar**
- **1 tbsp finely sliced red fresh chilli pepper**
- **5 tbsp fresh mint leaves, sliced if large**

1 Heat the oil in a wok and stir-fry the lamb for several minutes until almost cooked. Add the garlic, oyster sauce, Nuoc Mam sauce, sugar and chilli and stir-fry for another 2 minutes or so. Taste to see if extra seasoning is necessary and adjust.

2 When the meat is cooked and tender, stir the mint leaves through, remove and serve on a dish.

Stir-fried Lamb with Ginger

THIT CÙU XÀO VÓI GÙNG

SERVES 4

- **60ml/4 tbsp chicken stock**
- **1 medium carrot, diced into 1cm/½in cubes**
- **15g/½oz butter**
- **100g/4oz green peas**
- **1 tbsp vegetable oil**
- **2 slices root ginger, minced**
- **450g/1lb lean lamb, chopped into 1cm/½in cubes**
- **15ml/1 tbsp Nuoc Mam sauce or 15ml/1 tbsp Maggi liquid seasoning and 3ML/½ tsp anchovy essence**
- **1 tsp sugar**
- **8ml/½ tbsp hoisin sauce**
- **salt**
- **2 tsp cornflour mixed with a little water**

1 Heat the stock in a wok over a medium heat. Add the carrot and cook until the liquid has nearly disappeared. Add the butter and peas and leave to cook for a further 2 minutes, stirring occasionally. Scoop out and leave in a bowl.

2 Heat the oil in the wok on a high heat and add the ginger and lamb. Stir quickly for about 1 minute and then add the Nuoc Mam sauce, sugar, hoisin sauce and salt. Continue stirring for 1 minute and then stir in the cornflour.

3 When the cornflour thickens, it will give the lamb a beautiful gloss. At this stage add the carrots and peas. Stir and mix for 30 seconds and serve immediately.

Cold Crispy Roast Lamb, Beansprout and Bean Salad

THIT CÙU QUAY DÒN DÊ NGUÔI ĂN VÓI GIÁ VÀ DÂU

SERVES 4

- **100g/4oz crispy roast leg of lamb, thinly sliced and cut into 1 × 2.5cm/½ × 1in strips**
- **100g/4oz beansprouts, washed and dried**
- **100g/4oz French beans, tossed in boiling water for 5 minutes**
- **100g/4oz broccoli florets, blanched**
- **6 lettuce leaves, preferably Chinese**
- **3 large tomatoes, cut into wedges**
- **1 large cucumber, peeled and sliced**
- **½ medium sweet pepper, cut in strips**
- **2 medium-sized onions, finely sliced into rings**
- **6 spring onion curls**
- **3 hard-boiled eggs, peeled and halved**

DRESSING

- **75g/3oz unsalted roasted peanuts**
- **100ml/4fl oz lemon juice**
- **45ml/3 tbsp vinegar**
- **4 cloves garlic**
- **3 tbsp fresh coriander, chopped**
- **40g/1½oz sugar**
- **15ml/1 tbsp Nuoc Mam sauce or Maggi liquid seasoning**

GARNISH

- **1 hard-boiled egg, sliced**
- **fresh coriander, chopped**
- **chilli flowers (see page 16)**

1 Blend all the dressing ingredients in a blender using a little water to give you the consistency you want. Adjust by increasing vinegar, sugar or Nuoc Mam sauce. Set aside.

2 Arrange the salad ingredients on a large dish. Start off with a bed of lettuce and from there, you are on your own.

A typical sight: an overloaded passenger bus going to market.

The ubiquitous rickshaws transport goods as well as people.

Rice Dishes

Sticky Rice

XÔI

SERVES 4

In Vietnam sticky rice is often served at breakfast, which is convenient because the rice should be soaked for at least 8 hours. I know of two ways of preparing it and both are described below. Unlike Westerners, Vietnamese save the rice crust at the bottom of the saucepan for a variety of purposes: to dip in sauces, to deep-fry and to eat between meals in much the same way as Europeans eat biscuits.

- **400g/14oz glutinous rice (specified on packet)**
- **1 tsp salt**

METHOD 1

1 Rinse and drain the rice after soaking overnight. Spread the soaked rice mixed with the salt over a dampened cheesecloth in the top of a steamer and steam for about 40 minutes, sprinkling water over it occasionally. Taste while cooking for consistency. It should not be *al dente*; Vietnamese prefer it well boiled in much the same way the older generation in the United Kingdom prefer their vegetables well done.

METHOD 2

1 Boil about 700ml/1¼ pt water in a thick saucepan. Add the rice and salt and bring it back to the boil. Let it boil for 1 minute or so and then cover it with a well-fitting lid. Take it off the heat and hold the lid tightly on the saucepan. Turn it over and drain it fairly dry.

2 Return to a very low heat and allow the rice to cook for about 20 minutes. After cooking, set it aside for 10 minutes to complete the cooking. When ready to serve, fluff it up with a ladle or chopsticks, whichever you prefer.

A rice farmer tending a paddy field of young rice. Rice is the staple food of the Vietnamese and paddy fields are found throughout the country.

Egg Fried Rice

COM CHIÊN TRÚNG

SERVES 4

- **2 eggs**
- **30ml/2 tbsp water**
- **30ml/2 tbsp vegetable oil**
- **2 spring onions, finely chopped**
- **550g/1¼lb plain boiled rice**
- **30ml/2 tbsp soya sauce**
- **salt**
- **½ tsp sugar**

1 Beat the eggs with the water in a bowl. Heat 3ml/½ tsp oil in a wok and add the egg mixture. Swirl it around to make an omelette. Transfer to a plate and allow to cool. When cool, cut into strips.

2 Heat the remaining oil, add the spring onions and stir-fry for 2 minutes. Add the plain boiled rice and omelette strips.

3 Stir in the soya sauce, salt and sugar and cook for 2–3 minutes. Serve in a large bowl.

Perfumed Rice

COM GAO THOM

SERVES 4

Although some Thai rice is described as "perfumed" on the bag, most people are rightly unable to smell the touted fragrance. I believe this is just a marketing ploy dreamt up by astute businessmen. This is not to say that this particular rice does not have some merits. Indeed, most Vietnamese search for this rice as a matter of course because it is arguably the best rice in the world. My father belonged to this particular school and my experience is that it has always been a cut above other rice, even the famed basmati rice, which is slightly harder.

- ★ **400g/14oz Thai perfumed rice**
- ★ **600ml/1 pt water**
- ★ **1 tsp salt**

1 Wash the rice several times and drain; when the washing water is clear, the rice is as clean as it can possibly be. In large families rice needs washing with both hands but cooking for a nuclear family does not require more than the rubbing of rice between the fingers.

2 Put the rice and water in a saucepan, add the salt and bring quickly to the boil. Reduce the heat immediately and cover. Allow to simmer for as long as necessary – 30 minutes is about right. The rice should be taken off the heat and allowed to rest for about 10 minutes before serving. The result should be a rather moist, slightly sticky boiled rice that people east of the Ganges prefer.

Vegetable Rice

COM VÓI RAU

SERVES 4

The Chinese cabbage used here has dark green leaves and thick, succulent white stalks. It is one of the more delightful vegetables, looking not unlike spring onions but tasting a lot more delicious.

- ★ **400g/14oz short-grained rice, washed and drained**
- ★ **30ml/2 tbsp vegetable oil**
- ★ **450g/1lb pak-choy (Chinese cabbage), cut crossways in 2.5cm/1in pieces**
- ★ **salt**
- ★ **600–750ml/1–1¼ pt water**

1 Wash the rice several times until the water runs clear. Drain thoroughly.

2 Heat a heavy saucepan over a high heat. Add the oil, swirl and heat for a further 30 seconds or so. Add the cabbage and stir rapidly. The cabbage leaves should now be shiny with oil. Sprinkle some salt and stir and the leaves will brighten.

3 Put the rice and water in a saucepan and bring to the boil. Let it bubble for a couple of minutes, stirring occasionally. Turn the heat to medium and let it bubble for another 2 minutes, stirring occasionally.

4 Turn to the lowest possible heat, cover and let the rice cook for 20 minutes. When it is cooked, leave it to rest for 10 minutes before serving.

5 Lay the rice on a flat dish, placing the cabbage on top.

Prawn Fried Rice

COM CHIÊN VÓI TÔM

SERVES 4

- 30ml/2 tbsp vegetable oil
- 450g/1lb prawns, peeled
- 1 spring onion, chopped
- 50g/2oz fresh button mushrooms
- 1 courgette, thinly sliced
- ½ carrot, thinly sliced
- 50g/2oz French beans, cut into 2.5cm/1in lengths
- 15ml/1 tbsp rice wine or dry sherry
- 1 tsp light soya sauce
- freshly ground black pepper
- salt
- 550g/1¼lb plain boiled rice
- 2 spring onions, neatly chopped into rounds to garnish

1 Heat 8ml/½ tbsp oil in a wok and stir-fry the prawns for 1 minute. Remove and set aside.

2 Add the remaining oil and sweat the spring onion. Add the mushrooms and the other vegetables and stir-fry for 2 minutes over a high heat.

3 Put the prawns back into the wok with the vegetables and add the rest of the ingredients except the rice, continuing all the while to stir.

4 Add the rice and stir-fry until the rice has changed colour. Place in a large serving bowl and garnish with the chopped spring onions.

Prawn Fried Rice ▶

Plain Rice

COM THUÒNG

SERVES 4

- 400g/14oz long-grained white rice
- 600ml/1 pt water
- 1 tsp salt

1 Wash the rice several times until the water runs clear. Drain properly and add the water and salt. Bring to the boil. Turn down the heat until it is just bubbling gently. Cover with a lid and leave to cook for about 20 minutes. The Vietnamese believe that the way to cook perfect rice is never to lift the lid while it is boiling. After 20 minutes, lift the cover and test to see if the rice is done to perfection.

2 Turn off the heat, cover the saucepan once more and leave for about 10 minutes to give the rice time to absorb all the moisture.

VEGETABLE DISHES

Hot Egg and Shredded Vegetable Salad

RAU CÁT NHO TRÔN VÓI TRÚNG NÓNG THÁI NHO

SERVES 4

EGG PANCAKES

- ★ **2 eggs**
- ★ **¼ tsp Nuoc Mam sauce or light soya sauce**
- ★ **freshly ground black pepper**
- ★ **3ml/½ tsp water**
- ★ **15ml/1 tbsp vegetable oil**

- ★ **50g/2oz bean thread vermicelli**
- ★ **4 dried Chinese mushrooms**
- ★ **1 tbsp sesame seeds**
- ★ **2 cloves garlic, crushed**
- ★ **salt**
- ★ **2 tbsp rice vinegar**
- ★ **1½ tsp sugar**
- ★ **2 tbsp soya sauce**
- ★ **30ml/2 tbsp sesame oil**
- ★ **100g/4oz snow peas or mange tout peas, thinly sliced**
- ★ **50g/2oz bamboo shoots, thinly sliced**
- ★ **1 small carrot, peeled and thinly sliced**
- ★ **1 small daikon or white Chinese radish, peeled and thinly sliced**
- ★ **1 small cucumber, peeled, seeded and sliced thinly**
- ★ **1 small green bell pepper, thinly sliced**
- ★ **1 small red bell pepper, thinly sliced**
- ★ **2 celery stalks, thinly sliced**
- ★ **1 small red onion, thinly sliced**
- ★ **salt**
- ★ **1 tbsp roasted peanuts, ground**
- ★ **freshly ground black pepper**
- ★ **coriander sprigs**

1 Soak the vermicelli in warm water for 30 minutes, drain and cut into 5cm/2in lengths. Soak the dried Chinese mushrooms in warm water for 30 minutes, squeeze, discard the stems and slice thinly.

2 Make egg pancakes by beating together the eggs, Nuoc Mam sauce, black pepper and about 3ml/½ tsp water in a bowl. Heat the oil in a wok over a moderate heat. Pour in half of the egg mixture and immediately tilt the wok to spread the egg evenly over the bottom. The egg pancake should be crêpe-thin. Cook for about 30 seconds. Turn and cook on the other side for 15 seconds. Repeat with the rest of the mixture. Cool and cut into thin strips.

3 Toss the sesame seeds in a dry wok over a moderate heat. Stir constantly until golden brown. This should take about 3 minutes. Set aside.

4 Combine the garlic, salt, vinegar, sugar, soya sauce and sesame oil in a small bowl by stirring. Set this sauce aside.

5 Bring a saucepan of salted water to the boil and put in the noodles, snow peas, bamboo shoots and mushrooms and cook for 30 seconds. Drain into a colander immediately and run under a cold tap for a few seconds. Dry with a paper towel and set aside.

6 Mix the carrot, daikon, cucumber, bell peppers, celery and red onion in a bowl and sprinkle on some salt. Toss well and let stand for 30 minutes. Rinse the salt off and squeeze the vegetables dry by hand to remove all excess liquid and dry with kitchen paper to ensure the vegetables remain firm.

7 Combine all the shredded vegetables with the blanched vegetables in a large salad bowl. Sprinkle the sauce over the mixture. Toss well. Transfer the salad to a serving platter. Sprinkle the ground nuts and black pepper over the top and garnish with the egg pancake strips and coriander sprigs.

Vendors selling a green spring cabbage similar to Pak-Choy. Its delicate flavour makes it sought after, and so very expensive.

Stir-fried Mixed Vegetables in a Nuoc Mam Sauce

RAU THẬP CẨM XÀO VỚI NUỚC MẮM

SERVES 4

- **2 carrots, finely sliced**
- **100g/4oz bamboo shoots, thinly sliced**
- **1 pak-choy (Chinese cabbage), stems only, diced**
- **100g/4oz green beans, halved**
- **25g/1oz wood ear fungus, soaked in warm water for 15 minutes and roughly chopped**
- **3ml/½ tsp vegetable oil**
- **2 cloves garlic, crushed**
- **3 slices ginger, peeled and cut in slivers**
- **100g/4oz beansprouts**
- **salt**
- **freshly ground black pepper**
- **½ tbsp cornflour**
- **15ml/1 tbsp Nuoc Mam sauce or 15ml/1 tbsp light soya sauce**

1 In a large saucepan half full of water boil the carrots for 10 minutes. Add the bamboo shoots, Chinese cabbage, green beans and wood ear fungus and cook for a further 5 minutes. Drain and reserve.

2 Heat the oil in a wok and stir-fry the garlic and ginger for 2 minutes. Add the beansprouts and stir-fry for 30 seconds. Stir in all the reserved vegetables and season with salt and black pepper. Stir-fry for 2 minutes. Mix the cornflour and Nuoc Mam sauce with a little water and fold into the vegetables to bind them.

Green Peppers and Deep-fried Bean Curd

ỚT NGỌT XANH VỚI DẦU PHỤ CHIÊN

SERVES 4

- ★ 15ml/1 tbsp ground nut or corn oil
- ★ 2 thin slices fresh ginger, peeled
- ★ 4 large leaves Chinese celery cabbage, cut into 2.5cm/1in lengths
- ★ 1 large green bell pepper, seeded and sliced
- ★ salt
- ★ oil for deep-frying
- ★ 4 × 2.5cm/1in square cakes bean curd, drained and cut into rectangles, 3 per cake (use kitchen paper to drain)

SAUCE

- ★ 1 tsp potato flour
- ★ 75ml/5 tbsp mushroom water
- ★ 30ml/2 tbsp oyster sauce
- ★ 10ml/2 tsp thick soya sauce
- ★ 30ml/2 tbsp vegetable oil
- ★ 1 clove garlic, finely chopped
- ★ 2 spring onions, cut into 2.5cm/1in sections, white and green parts separated
- ★ 4 large dried Chinese mushrooms, soaked, squeezed and cut into thin strips (water to be reserved)

1 Prepare the sauce by mixing together the potato flour, mushroom water, oyster sauce and soya sauce. Heat a wok and add 30ml/2 tbsp oil and swirl around. Add the garlic, letting it sizzle and then add the white spring onion and then the Chinese mushrooms. Stir for about 30 seconds and pour in the potato flour mixture. Lower the heat and continue to stir until the sauce thickens. Remove from heat.

2 Heat 15ml/1 tbsp nut or corn oil in a wok over a high heat until it starts to smoke. Add the ginger and when it starts to sizzle, add the cabbage and green pepper. Toss for about 30 seconds. Season with a little salt, lower the heat and continue to cook, covered for a further 2 minutes. Remove and put into an earthenware pot or saucepan.

3 Now half fill the wok with oil, heat to 100°C/200°F and lower the bean curd into the oil, one piece at a time, and deep-fry for 4 minutes or until golden brown, turning over from time to time. Remove with a large strainer and drain on kitchen paper.

4 Lay the bean curd on the cabbage in the pot and add the green spring onion. Heat the sauce and pour this over the bean curd. Heat the pot for 2 minutes and serve.

Shan Lee Salad

MÓN TRỘN SHAN LEE

SERVES 4

This salad was created by a great Vietnamese friend of my father's. It is remarkable for its simplicity.

- ★ 45ml/3 tbsp sesame seed oil
- ★ 45ml/3 tbsp freshly squeezed orange juice
- ★ 1 Webbs or round lettuce, the leaves washed and separated
- ★ 60ml/4 tbsp bamboo shoots

1 Mix the sesame oil and orange juice together and toss into the salad leaves and bamboo shoots. Serve as a simple accompaniment to the Saté dishes (pages 36–38) or Stuffed Chicken Wings (page 58).

French Beans with Crushed Garlic

DÂU PHÁP VỚI TOI NGHIÊN

SERVES 4

- 15ml/1 tbsp vegetable oil
- 1 onion, finely chopped
- 4 cloves garlic, finely chopped
- 3 large green chillies, de-seeded and sliced thinly diagonally
- 1 tsp ground coriander
- ½ tsp ground cumin
- 2 ripe tomatoes, blanched, skinned, de-seeded and chopped roughly
- 450g/1lb French beans, washed, trimmed and halved
- ½ tsp sugar
- pinch of salt
- 2 tbsp fresh coriander, chopped

1 Heat the oil in a wok and stir-fry the onion, garlic and green chillies, stirring constantly, for 2 minutes.

2 Add the coriander and cumin, stir vigorously and add the chopped tomatoes and French beans. Stir and cover the wok for 5 minutes. Remove the cover, add the sugar and a little salt, and stir again for 1 minute. Add the coriander, stir for 30 seconds and transfer to a warm serving dish.

Spicy Aubergines and Tomatoes

Cà Tím Gia Vi Vói Cà Chua

SERVES 4

- **1 aubergine**
- **2 cloves garlic, thinly sliced**
- **2 red bell peppers**
- **1 medium tomato, thinly sliced**
- **15ml/1 tbsp Nuoc Mam sauce or 15ml/1 tbsp Maggi liquid seasoning and 3ml/½ tsp anchovy essence**
- **30ml/2 tbsp rice wine**
- **15ml/1 tbsp olive oil**

1 Preheat the oven to 200°C/400°F/Gas Mark 6.

2 Cut slits all over the aubergine and push a slice of garlic into each slit. Place the aubergine and the whole bell peppers in a baking dish and bake, turning regularly to brown evenly, for 45 minutes or until all are very soft. Set aside to cool.

3 Cut the stem off the aubergine and with your fingers or a paring knife, peel off the skin. Shred the flesh, discarding any big lumps of seeds. Place the aubergine in a bowl with the garlic slices.

4 Peel the skin off the bell peppers and discard the stems, cores and seeds. Cut into long, thin strips and add to the aubergine. Add the tomato, Nuoc Mam sauce, rice wine and olive oil and toss to mix well.

NOODLES

Spicy Fried Noodles

MÌ XÀO GIA VỊ

SERVES 4

You can make your own chilli powder by roasting 100g/4oz red chilli peppers in the oven at 200°C/400°F/Gas Mark 6 until brown. Blend briefly if you want flakes. Process more for powder. Store in an airtight container.

- ★ **30ml/2tbsp vegetable oil**
- ★ **2 cloves garlic, finely chopped**
- ★ **100g/4oz pork, sliced**
- ★ **4 large uncooked prawns, peeled, deveined, tails intact**
- ★ **1 tbsp dried shrimp**
- ★ **2 tbsp pickled white radish, finely chopped**
- ★ **50g/2oz bean curd, diced**
- ★ **45ml/3 tbsp lemon juice**
- ★ **45ml/3 tbsp Nuoc Mam sauce or light soya sauce and 3ml/½ tsp anchovy essence**
- ★ **40g/1½oz sugar**
- ★ **175g/6oz rice stick noodles (preferably the thicker ones), soaked in warm water for 15 minutes and drained well**
- ★ **2 eggs, beaten**
- ★ **50g/2oz beansprouts**
- ★ **3 tbsp crushed peanuts**
- ★ **2 tbsp chopped spring onions**
- ★ **2 tbsp chopped fresh coriander**

GARNISH

- ★ **½ tsp roasted chilli powder or flakes**
- ★ **lemon wedges**

1 Heat the oil in a wok and gently stir-fry the garlic for 3–4 minutes until golden brown. Increase the heat, add the pork and fry for 6 minutes until cooked. Add the prawns, dried shrimp and pickled radish and continue stir-frying for 1 minute. Add the bean curd, stir, reduce the heat and add the lemon juice, Nuoc Mam sauce and sugar, stirring all the while for 3 minutes.

2 Add the noodles and stir the mixture thoroughly for 1–2 minutes. Push to one side and quickly add the beaten eggs. Once they begin to set, stir them, effectively scrambling them. Push to one side.

3 Place most of the beansprouts and a handful of crushed peanuts, spring onions and coriander over the noodles. Stir these in with the scrambled eggs and noodles. Serve on a large plate with little mounds of beansprouts, peanuts, spring onion, coriander, chilli flakes and lemon wedges.

A covered market. The main produce for sale would be fish, fruit and vegetables.

Stir-fried Noodles and Beansprouts

MÌ XÀO VỚI GIÁ

SERVES 4

- **15ml/1 tbsp vegetable oil**
- **2 small onions, thinly sliced**
- **4 cloves garlic, chopped**
- **100g/4oz beansprouts**
- **175g/6oz (dried weight) cellophane noodles, soaked in warm water for 30 minutes, drained and cut into 7.5cm/3in lengths**
- **100m/4 fl oz chicken stock**
- **15ml/1 tbsp Nuoc Mam sauce or light soya sauce**
- **2 spring onions, thinly sliced**
- **1 tbsp fresh coriander, chopped**
- **freshly ground black pepper**

1 Heat the oil in a wok over high heat. Add the onions and garlic and sauté for 2 minutes or so until the edges begin to brown.

2 Add the beansprouts and stir-fry for 30 seconds. Add the noodles and stir-fry for 1 minute. Stir in the chicken stock and Nuoc Mam sauce and toss to combine. Add the spring onions and remove from heat. Serve on a serving dish with coriander and black pepper sprinkled all over.

Ho Chi Minh City's town hall displays the colonial-style French architecture to be found in Vietnam.

Stir-fried Vermicelli with Vegetables

MÍ BÙN XÀO VÓI RAU DÂU

SERVES 4

- **15ml/1 tbsp vegetable oil**
- **1 clove garlic, finely chopped**
- **1 carrot, thinly sliced**
- **50ml/2fl oz water**
- **50g/2oz pak-choy (Chinese cabbage), shredded**
- **½ celery stick, shredded**
- **45ml/3 tbsp chicken stock**
- **15ml/1 tbsp oyster sauce**
- **15ml/1 tbsp Nuoc Mam sauce or 15ml/1 tbsp light soya sauce and ½ tsp anchovy essence**
- **1 level tsp sugar**
- **freshly ground black pepper**
- **100ml/4oz rice vermicelli, soaked in warm water for 5 minutes and drained well**

1 Heat the oil in a wok over high heat and fry the garlic until golden brown. Add the carrot and stir-fry for 1 minute.

2 Add all the remaining ingredients except the vermicelli, stirring gently. Cook for 2 minutes.

3 Add the vermicelli and toss to combine all the ingredients. Stir for 1 minute. Serve in a large serving dish.

Rice Vermicelli and Egg

BÚN XÀO TRÚNG

SERVES 4

- **50g/2oz rice vermicelli**
- **1 tsp black jack**
- **2 cloves garlic, crushed**
- **2 spring onions, roughly chopped**
- **salt and freshly ground black pepper**
- **6 eggs, beaten**
- **1 iceberg lettuce, shredded**
- **½ cucumber, sliced**
- **2 tbsp pickled carrots or gherkins**
- **1 tbsp chopped fresh mint leaves**
- **1 tbsp chopped fresh coriander**
- **15ml/1 tbsp vegetable oil**

NUOC MAM GIAM SAUCE

- **1 clove garlic, roughly chopped**
- **1 fresh red chilli pepper, roughly chopped**
- **15ml/1 tbsp Nuoc Mam sauce or 15ml/1 tbsp Maggi sauce and 5ml/ 1 tsp anchovy essence**
- **5ml/1 tsp lemon juice or vinegar**
- **15g/½ oz sugar**

1 To prepare the rice vermicelli, bring a large saucepan of salted water to the boil. Add the rice vermicelli and boil, stirring constantly to separate the vermicelli, for about 3 minutes. It should be tender but firm to the bite. Drain in a colander and rinse under cold running water to stop the cooking. Set aside.

2 Make the Nuoc Mam Giam sauce by grinding the garlic and chilli together in a blender or, better still, pound in a mortar with a pestle. Transfer to a small bowl. Stir in the other ingredients and mix thoroughly, making sure that the sugar dissolves.

3 Make some black jack if you cannot find any in the supermarket. Heat 15g/½oz sugar in a wok until it darkens. Remove from the heat and carefully stir in 30ml/2 tbsp cold water. Do this extremely carefully or you will finish up with burns on your hand. Save whatever is left over in refrigerator.

4 Combine the garlic, spring onions and black jack in a shallow dish and add salt and black pepper and the beaten eggs. Mix well and set aside to marinate for a few minutes.

5 Set out the lettuce, cucumber, pickled vegetables, mint and coriander into 4 individual bowls. Top each portion of vegetables with cooked vermicelli. Set aside.

6 Heat the oil in a wok and pour in the egg mixture. Flip it over once and let it cool for 1–2 minutes in a dish. Cut into 8 pieces. Put 2 pieces in each individual bowl and top each with 30ml/2 tbsp Nuoc Mam Giam sauce. The guests mix the contents of their bowls.

A "fast food" vendor. It is commonplace to sit and eat on the roadside, enjoying the sights and smells.

DESSERTS

Lychee Slap

TRÁI VAI DÂP

SERVES 4

My father invented this quick, easy and delightful dessert. I have often used it when in a hurry.

- **1 medium jar Chinese stem ginger, drained**
- **100g/4oz can lychees**
- **15ml/1tbsp ginger wine**

1 Insert a piece of the drained stem ginger into each lychee.

2 Mix the liquid from the stem ginger and the lychee syrup and add the ginger wine. Pour over the stuffed lychees.

Lychee and Ginger Ice

KEM TRÁI VAI VỚI GÙNG

SERVES 4

- **100g/4oz lychees in heavy syrup**
- **15g/½oz root ginger, peeled and grated**
- **150ml/¼ pt water**

GARNISH

- **fresh mint leaves**
- **lychees**
- **sponge ginger biscuits (optional)**

1 Put the lychees in a blender or food processor together with the ginger and water and process to a fine purée. Pour the mixture into a 23cm/9in square baking tin and and put into the freezer for 3 hours.

2 Break the iced mixture into chunks and process again until slushy. Return to the baking tin and freeze once more until solid.

3 Allow the mixture to soften slightly (about 5 minutes) and scoop into 4 champagne glasses or rice bowls. Garnish with mint leaves, lychees and a biscuit, if desired.

Lychee Sorbet

TRÁI VAI DĂ LÂY HÔT

SERVES 4

This is a really simple and refreshing sorbet which is quick and easy to make.

- **450g/1lb fresh lychees or 100g/4oz can lychees**
- **1 egg white**

1 Peel the lychees and stone them. Liquidize the flesh, adding some sugared water if necessary. Pour into a container and freeze until nearly set.

2 Whip up the egg white. Mix this into the nearly set lychee mixture. Put back into the freezer until solid.

An awesome, serene statue of Buddha.

Coconut Custard

CHÈ DÙA

SERVES 4

- **225ml/8oz thick coconut cream**
- **4 eggs, beaten**
- **100g/4oz sugar**

1 Beat the coconut cream, eggs and sugar together until the sugar dissolves and the mixture is thoroughly blended. Sieve the mixture through muslin. The result should be perfectly smooth.

2 Place a serving bowl on top of a wooden trivet in a wok and test it for firmness. Pour the mixture into the serving bowl. Pour some water into the wok and bring to the boil. Place the serving bowl on the wooden trivet and allow to steam until the mixture is firm – about 10–15 minutes.

3 Alternatively, pour the mixture into 4 individual bowls and steam in a large bamboo steamer.

Coconut Ice Cream

KEM DÙA

SERVES 4

- ★ 275ml/10fl oz thick coconut milk
- ★ 350ml/12fl oz fresh cream
- ★ 2 eggs
- ★ 2 egg yolks
- ★ 5ml/1 tsp vanilla essence
- ★ 100g/4oz sugar
- ★ salt

GARNISH

- ★ 50g/2oz desiccated coconut, dry-fried until golden brown
- ★ sprigs of mint

1 Heat the coconut milk and cream over a medium heat and cook for 5 minutes without boiling over. Beat together the eggs, egg yolks, vanilla, sugar and salt.

2 Place a deep bowl in a saucepan with boiling water up to the halfway mark of the bowl. Pour in the egg mixture and beat in the warm coconut milk mixture, a little at a time. Stir until the mixture thickens enough to coat a spoon. Remove from the heat, stirring occasionally as it cools.

3 Pour into a bowl when it is cool enough to be put into the freezer. Freeze for 1 hour. Scoop out into a blender or food processor and process until smooth. Pour back into the bowl and freeze until solid.

4 Serve in scoops, garnished with desiccated coconut and sprigs of mint.

Banana and Pineapple Fritters

CHUÔI VÀ DÚA CHIÊN NGOT

SERVES 4

- ★ vegetable oil for deep-frying
- ★ 4 bananas, peeled and halved lengthways
- ★ 4 pineapple rings, fresh or canned, dried on absorbent kitchen paper
- ★ icing sugar, sieved

BATTER

- ★ 50g/2oz self-raising flour
- ★ 150g/5oz plain flour
- ★ ½ tsp baking powder
- ★ 30ml/2 tbsp vegetable oil
- ★ salt
- ★ 1 egg white, beaten until stiff

1 Make the batter first. Mix the flours, baking powder, salt and oil in a large bowl. Stir in just enough water to make a smooth paste. Fold in the egg white a little at a time.

2 Heat some oil in a wok for deep-frying. Dip the fruit in the batter and cook in small batches (do not put more than can comfortably float on the oil) until puffy and golden. This should not take more than 2 minutes.

3 Drain the cooked fritters on absorbent kitchen paper and sprinkle with the sieved icing sugar. Serve while hot.

One of the beautiful tranquil waterways of Southern Vietnam.

Mango Ice Cream

Kem Xoài

SERVES 4

- 4 ripe mangoes or 100g/4oz can sliced mango
- 225g/8oz sugar or 100g/4oz if using canned mango
- 15ml/1 tbsp lemon juice
- 1 tbsp gelatine, dissolved in 45ml/3 tbsp water
- 350ml/12fl oz double cream, whipped until stiff

GARNISH

- extra mango slices
- sprigs of fresh mint

1 Peel and cut the mangoes, discarding the stones. Place in a bowl and add the sugar, lemon juice and dissolved gelatine. Mix thoroughly, making sure that the sugar is dissolved.

2 Fold the whipped cream into the mango mixture. Spoon into a tray and put into the freezer until half-frozen. Put in a blender or food processor and process until smooth. Return to freezer and freeze until solid.

3 Serve in scoops garnished with freshly sliced mango and sprigs of fresh mint.

Mango Ice Cream ▶

Ginger Surprise

Bánh Gùng Dăc Biêt

SERVES 4

- 25g/1oz root ginger, crushed
- 225g/8oz sugar
- 350ml/12fl oz hot water

FILLING

- 50g/2oz dried yellow mung beans, soaked in warm water for 30 minutes and drained
- 20g/¾oz sugar
- 4 tbsp sesame seeds

DOUGH

- 225g/8oz glutinous rice flour or ordinary flour
- 175ml/8fl oz boiling water

1 Make the ginger syrup by swirling the ginger and sugar constantly in a small saucepan over low heat, until the sugar browns. When it starts to smoke, stir in the hot water (be careful: you could give yourself a nasty burn with the spluttering) and allow to boil for about 3 minutes until the sugar is dissolved. Set aside in a cool place. Discard the ginger when cooled.

2 Make the filling by steaming the mung beans over high heat for 20 minutes. Transfer to a blender or food processor, add the sugar and process to a fine paste. Put in the refrigerator for 20 minutes to firm up.

3 Toast the sesame seeds by dry-frying in a wok for 2 minutes. Reserve 2 tbsp for garnishing, put the remainder in a blender and process to a paste. Combine with the mung bean paste and blend well. Roll 16 marble-sized balls of the mixture (1 tsp each). Set aside.

4 Place the glutinous rice flour in a mixing bowl and quickly mix with the hot water to make a sticky dough. Cover and leave to stand for 5 minutes. Dust a work surface with flour and knead the dough for 3 minutes until soft and smooth. Divide into 2 equal parts. Roll each into a rope about 25cm/10in long and 25cm/1in in diameter. Cut each into 10 equal portions and roll each one into a ball. Cover with a damp cloth.

5 Flatten the dough balls, one at a time, into 6cm/2½in discs. Place a mung bean ball in the centre, gather the edges around and pinch to seal. Roll the dumplings between the palms to form perfect balls.

6 Divide each of the remaining four dough balls into four, cover and set aside.

7 Bring a large pot of water to the boil. Boil the filled dumplings for 2 minutes over a moderate heat. Add the smaller dumplings and cook for a further 3 minutes or until they rise to the surface. Drain.

8 Reheat the ginger syrup over low heat in a large saucepan. Add the dumplings and allow to simmer for 2 minutes. Set aside to cool.

9 Serve four large dumplings and four small ones to each person in individual dessert cups or rice bowls. Sprinkle with the reserved toasted sesame seeds.

Bananas in a Rich Coconut Sauce

CHUÔI VỚI NƯỚC CỐT DỪA

SERVES 4

- **350ml/12fl oz coconut milk**
- **20g/¾oz sugar**
- **salt**
- **6 large bananas, peeled and sliced diagonally about 2cm/¾in thick**
- **ice cream or whipped cream to serve**

1 Heat the coconut milk in a small saucepan and add the sugar and salt. Bring to the boil. Lower the heat and simmer for 2 minutes.

2 Remove from the heat and stir in the banana slices. Bring back to the boil for a few seconds to coat the bananas. Serve with ice cream or whipped cream.

INDEX

A

aubergine
- Sautéed Lamb with Aubergine in a Sauce 95
- Steamed Minced Pork with Aubergine 84
- Spicy Aubergines & Tomatoes 111

B

bamboo shoots 18
- Stir-fried Beef with Peppers & Bamboo Shoots 91

bananas
- Banana & Pineapple Fritters 123
- Bananas in a Rich Coconut Sauce 126
- Deep Fried Squid with Plantain/Banana Fritters 51
- Fried Frogs' Legs with Banana 74

Banh Pho 18
Banh Trang 18
Banh Xeo Stuffed with Minced Pork & Beansprouts 42
Bass, Grilled, with Ginger Sauce 47
bean curd 18
- Green Peppers & Deep Fried Bean Curd 109
- Quail's Eggs with Bean Curd & Vegetables

Beansprouts
- Banh Xeo Stuffed with Minced Pork & Beansprouts 42
- Cold Crispy Roast Lamb, Beansprouts & Bean Salad 98
- Stir-fried Noodles & Beansprouts 114

beef
- Beef in Coconut Milk 87
- Beef Crystal Spring Rolls 30, *31*
- Beef & French Fries 93
- Beef with Lemon Grass & Mushrooms 90
- Beef Pho 26
- Beef Saté 36
- Crispy Beef Slices Served with a Spicy Dip 92
- French Colonial Steak 90
- Minced Meat, Crab & Grapefruit Vietnamese Salad 39
- Spicy Beef Stew 88, *89*
- Spicy Beef Stew II 88
- Stir-fried Beef with Peppers & Bamboo Shoots 91

black beans 18
black vinegar 18
Boiled Chicken with Nuoc Mam Sauce 65
breakfast 17
Brown Stock 23

C

Caramelized Chicken Wings with an Orange Sauce 57
Carp Cooked in Coconut Milk 48
carrot, as garnish 15–16
Cashew Nuts, Fresh Chicken with Lemon Grass & 62
Casserole of Duck with Dumplings 71
Celery, & Stir-fried Pork Slices 83
chicken
- Boiled Chicken with Nuoc Mam Sauce 65
- Caramelized Chicken Wings with an Orange Sauce 57
- Chicken with Mango 63
- Chicken Pho 36
- Chicken Porridge 64
- Chicken Saté 36
- Chicken Stock 23
- Fresh Chicken with Lemon Grass & Cashew Nuts 62
- Fresh Chicken Salad with Grapefruit, Mint & Lemon Grass 60
- Jellyfish, Chicken & Cucumber Salad 55
- jointing a chicken 12
- Poulet Citron 66
- Spicy Barbecued Chicken Legs 59
- Stewed Chicken Feet with a Mushroom & Spring Onion Sauce 66
- Stuffed Chicken Wings 58

chillies 19
- as garnish 16
- ground chilli 20

chopping block 10
cleaver, using 10–13
coconut custard 122
coconut milk 19
- Beef in Coconut Milk 87
- Carp Cooked in Coconut Milk 48

Cold Crispy Roast Lamb, Beansprouts & Bean Salad 98
coriander, ground 20
coriander leaves 19
coriander root 19
Corn, & Crab Porridge 43
crab
- Crab & Corn Porridge 43
- Minced Meat, Crab & Grapefruit Vietnamese Salad 39
- Steamed Crab with Light Wine Sauce 48
- Stir-fried Seafood with Mint, Garlic & Chillies 53
- Stuffed Crab with Minced Pork & Coriander 52

Crispy Beef Slices Served with a Spicy Dip 92
Crispy Roast Duck with Pancakes & Fresh Herbs 70
cucumbers, as garnish 16
cumin 19

D

Deep Fried Fish Cakes 44
Deep Fried Squid with Plantain/Banana Fritters 51
duck
- Casserole of Duck with Dumplings 71
- Crispy Roast Duck with Pancakes & Fresh Herbs 70
- Duck with Ginger Sauce 68
- Garlic Roasted Duck 67

Dumplings, Casserole of Duck with 71

E

Eel, Fried, with Lemon Grass & Peanut 47
Egg, Hot, & Shredded Vegetable Salad 107
Egg, Rice Vermicelli & 117
Egg Fried Rice 102
Egg Pancakes 60

F

fish
- Carp Cooked in Coconut Milk 48
- Deep Fried Fish Cakes 44
- Fish Crystal Spring Rolls 30
- Fish Stock 23
- Fried Eel with Lemon Grass & Peanut 47
- Grilled Bass with Ginger Sauce 47
- Mackerel Cooked in a Pot Lined with Belly Pork 54
- Stir-fried Seafood with Mint, Garlic & Chillies 52

five-spice powder 19
French Beans with Crushed Garlic 110
French Colonial Steak 90
Fritters, Banana & Pineapple 123
Fritters, Plantain/Banana with Deep Fried Squid 51
Fresh Chicken with Lemon Grass & Cashew Nuts 62
Fresh Chicken Salad with Grapefruit, Mint & Lemon Grass 60
Frogs' Legs, Fried, with Banana 74
Frogs' Legs, Fried, with Garlic Sauce 74, *75*

G

galangal 19
Garlic Roasted Duck 67
garnishes 14–16
ginger, Chinese stem 19
Ginger Surprise 124
grapefruit
- Fresh Chicken Salad with Grapefruit, Mint & Lemon Grass 60
- Minced Meat, Crab & Grapefruit Vietnamese Salad 39

Green Peppers & Deep Fried Bean Curd 109
Grilled Bass with Ginger Sauce 47
Grilled Pigs' Trotters 81

H

hoisin sauce 20
Hot Egg & Shredded Vegetable Salad 107

I

ices
- Coconut Ice Cream 123
- Lychee & Ginger Ice 120
- Lychee Sorbet 121
- Mango Ice Cream 124, *125*

J

Jellyfish, Chicken & Cucumber Salad 55
jellyfish, dried 19

L

lamb
- Cold Crispy Roast Lamb, Beansprout & Bean Salad 98
- Lamb in Hot Garlic Sauce 96, *97*
- Lamb's Liver with Ginger & Coriander 96
- Sautéed Lamb with Aubergine in a Sauce 95
- Stir-fried Lamb with Ginger 98
- Stir-fried Lamb with Mint & Chilli 98

lemon grass 20
Lobster & Sweet Potato Curry 53
Lu Soy 21
Lychee & Ginger Ice 120
Lychee Slap 119
Lychee Sorbet 121

M

Mackerel Cooked in a Pot Lined with Belly Pork 54
Mango, Chicken with 63
Mango Ice Cream 124, *125*
Marinated Quail in Honey 72
mealtimes 17
meat, slicing & shredding 13–14
Minced Meat, Crab & Grapefruit Vietnamese Salad 39
Minced Pork, Prawn & Pineapple Salad with a Fish Sauce Dressing 78
mincing technique 11, 13
Mushroom Saté 38

mushrooms, Chinese 19
mushrooms, straw 21

N
noodles 20
- bean thread vermicelli 18
- rice vermicelli 20
- Rice Vermicelli & Egg 117
- Spicy Fried Noodles 113
- Spicy Grilled Pork on a Bed of Vermicelli 85
- Stir-fried Noodles & Beansprouts 114
- Stir-fried Vermicelli with Vegetables 116

Nuoc Mam Sauce 6, 17, 20

O
oranges, as garnish 16
oyster sauce 20

P
Pancake, Vietnamese 40
Pancakes, Egg 66
paprika 20
peppers
- Green Peppers & Deep Fried Bean Curd 109
- Stir-fried Beef with Peppers & Bamboo Shoots 91
- Spicy Aubergines & Tomatoes 111

Perfumed Rice 103
Pig Trotter Stew 81
pineapples
- Banana & Pineapple Fritters 123
- Minced Pork, Prawn & Pineapple Salad with a Fish Sauce Dressing 78

Plantain Fritters, Deep Fried Squid with 51
pomelo 20
pork
- Fresh Chicken Salad with Grapefruit, Mint & Lemon Grass 60
- Banh Xeo Stuffed with Minced Pork & Beansprouts 42
- Crab Stuffed with Minced Pork & Coriander 52
- Grilled Pigs' Trotters 81
- Mackerel Cooked in a Pot Lined with Belly Pork 54
- Minced Meat, Crab & Grapefruit Vietnamese Salad 39
- Minced Pork, Prawn & Pineapple Salad with a Fish Sauce Dressing 78
- Prawn Crystal Spring Rolls 28
- Prawn & Minced Pork on Sugar Cane 34
- Pig Trotter Stew 81
- Pork Knuckle & Peanut Stew 82
- Roasted Spare Ribs with Lemon Grass & Chilli 45
- Spicy Grilled Pork on a Bed of Vermicelli 85
- Steamed Minced Pork & Aubergine 84
- Steamed Minced Pork with Saltfish 77
- Stir-fried Pork Slices & Celery 83
- Stuffed Chicken Wings 58
- Stuffed Roast Suckling Pig 82
- Vietnamese Pork au Caramel 80

Poulet Citron 66
poultry, jointing 12
prawns
- Fresh Chicken Salad with Grapefruit, Mint & Lemon Grass 60
- Minced Pork, Prawn & Pineapple Salad with a Fish Sauce Dressing 78
- Prawn Balls 26
- Prawn Crystal Spring Rolls 28
- Prawn Fried Rice 104, *105*
- Prawn & Minced Pork on Sugar Cane 34
- Prawn Pho 26
- Prawn & Scallop Saté 37
- Prawns with Sesame Seeds on Toast 25
- Stir-fried Seafood with Mint, Garlic & Chillies 52

Q
Quail, Marinated, in Honey 72
Quail's Eggs with Bean Curd & Vegetables 73

R
rice
- Egg Fried Rice 102
- Perfumed Rice 103
- Plain Rice 104
- Prawn Fried Rice 104
- Rice Vermicelli & Egg 117
- Sticky Rice 101
- Vegetable Rice 103

Roasted Spare Ribs with Lemon Grass & Chilli 45

S
sake 20
saltfish 20
- Steamed Minced Pork with Saltfish 77

salads
- Cold Crispy Roast Lamb, Beansprouts & Bean Salad 98
- Fresh Chicken Salad with Grapefruit, Mint & Lemon Grass 60
- Hot Egg & Shredded Vegetable Salad 107
- Jellyfish, Chicken & Cucumber Salad 55
- Minced Meat, Crab & Grapefruit Vietnamese Salad 39
- Shan Lee Salad 109
- Simple Salad 40, *41*
- Vietnamese Salad 38

Saté
- Beef 36
- Chicken 36
- Mushroom 38
- Prawn & Scallop 37

Sautéed Lamb with Aubergine in a Sauce 95
scallops
- Prawn & Scallop Saté 37
- Scallops Grilled in Pork Fat with Nuoc Mam Sauce 50
- Scallops Stuffed with Shrimp Paste 49

Sesame Seeds, Prawns with, on Toast 25
Shan Lee Salad 109
Shrimp Paste, Scallops Stuffed with 49
Simple Salad 109
slicing technique 13
soya sauce 21
Spicy Aubergines & Tomatoes 111
Spicy Barbecued Chicken Legs 59
Spicy Beef Stew 88, *89*
Spicy Beef Stew II 88
Spicy Fried Noodles 113
Spicy Grilled Pork on a Bed of Vermicelli 85
spring onion, as garnish 14
spring rolls
- Beef Crystal Spring Rolls 30
- Fish Crystal Spring Rolls 30
- Prawn Crystal Spring Rolls 28
- Vegetarian Crystal Vietnamese Rolls 33
- Vegetarian Vietnamese Spring Rolls 35
- Vietnamese Spring Rolls 32–3

squid
- Deep Fried Squid with Plantain/Banana Fritters 51
- Stir-fried Seafood with Mint, Garlic & Chillies 52

star anise 19, 21
Steamed Minced Pork with Aubergine 84
Steamed Minced Pork with Saltfish 77
steamers, bamboo 10
Stewed Chicken Feet with Mushroom & Spring Onion Sauce 66
Sticky Rice 101
Stir-fried Beef with Peppers & Bamboo Shoots 91
Stir-fried Lamb with Ginger 98
Stir-fried Lamb with Mint & Chilli 98
Stir-fried Mixed Vegetables in a Nuoc Mam Sauce 108
Stir-fried Noodles & Beansprouts 114
Stir-fried Pork Slices & Celery 83
Stir-fried Seafood with Mint, Garlic & Chillies 52
Stir-fried Vermicelli with Vegetables 116
stock 23
strainer, bamboo 10
Stuffed Chicken Wings 58
Stuffed Roast Suckling Pig 82
sugar cane 21
- Prawn & Minced Pork on Sugar Cane 34

Sweet Potato Curry, Lobster & 53
Szechwan peppercorns 21

T
turmeric 21

U
utensils 8–11

V
Vegetable Rice 103
Vegetable Stock 23
Vegetarian Crystal Vietnamese Rolls 33
vermicelli
- bean thread 18
- rice 20
- Rice Vermicelli & Egg 117
- Spicy Grilled Pork on a Bed of Vermicelli 86
- Stir-fried Vermicelli with Vegetables 116

Vietnamese Pancake 40
Vietnamese Pork au Caramel 80
Vietnamese Salad 38
Vietnamese Spring Rolls 32–3
Vietnamese Vegetarian Spring Rolls 35

W
wok 8–9
wok brush 10
wok scoop 10
wok stand 9–10
wood ear fungus 21

Y
yellow bean sauce 21